THE
OPEN
END
OF
CHRISTIAN
MORALS

# The Open End

Books by Wesley C. Baker
Published by The Westminster Press

THE OPEN END OF CHRISTIAN MORALS
MORE THAN A MAN CAN TAKE, A STUDY OF JOB
THE SPLIT-LEVEL FELLOWSHIP

of Christian Morals

ADULTS ONLY.
NO ONE
WILL BE
SEATED AFTER
THE FIRST
CHAPTER.

*177*

BY WESLEY C. BAKER

*Philadelphia*

*The Westminster Press*

Library of Congress Catalog Card No. 67–15087

Published by The Westminster Press ®
Philadelphia, Pennsylvania

PRINTED IN THE UNITED STATES OF AMERICA

*To Angelina*

# CONTENTS

# FOREWORD

THEY SAID to me, " Pastor, tell us about the new ideas of morality." I said, " They're not so new; it's what we've been talking about all the time." They said, " You'd better tell us again."

So I spoke and preached and seminared and discussed, and we reasoned together. We read and underlined many of the current books on the subject. And they scratched their heads. And they said, " You'd better write that down."

So I wrote it, and Wilma Grant made it legible, and we all hope it's readable.

W. C. B.

*San Rafael, California*

# A MARITIME PARABLE

A SHIP sets sail from San Francisco to Tokyo. As it glides under the Golden Gate Bridge, the captain comes on the speaker system to address the crew. "Men, you know that the rules of the sea have always directed that the word of the captain is authoritative and unquestionable, and that the one supreme law for the sailor is to obey."

So what else is new? He might as well have come on with the grand announcement that the water is wet and that if we're all good boys, we'll have some free time ashore in Japan. So quoth the world at rules of law. But the old man on the bridge isn't through.

"However, my idea of running a ship is different. More than wanting to get this cargo safely to its destination, I am interested in you as persons."

How corny can you get? We're here to get a certain job done, not to organize a mutual admiration society. The old guy's off his rocker before we've even dropped the pilot!

"So here is the way this voyage will go. Instead of following a book of clearly stated rules that describe your duties and prescribe beyond question what you must do on all occasions, you are to relate to me and to each other in respect, and together we will appraise every shipboard decision, and your word will have power."

That's about as loony a way to run a ship as there is! Captains are to give orders, and crews are to obey, so that there is one definite course, one solid administration, and everybody is secure in knowing his place. So the skipper is going to let us run the ship "in respect." Ye gods!

The first major snarl comes almost immediately. The captain walks into the wheelhouse, and the yeoman at the wheel asks the course. Instead of giving the usual compass figure, the captain says: "You're at the wheel. What do you think?" In panic the seaman, eyes bugging out, groans, "You're putting me on, skipper!"

But the captain is very serious. "Look," he says quietly, "you know a little about the sea; you've been at the wheel of other ships before. You know we're going to Japan and you know how to read a chart and a weather report. You also know that you have the lives and welfare of sixty men in your hands at that wheel. I'm giving you complete freedom to make the choice of course, and I will trust and respect you, no matter what your decision is."

The young man, at first elated because of the officer's confidence in him, then a little arrogant because of the great power that has been delivered into his hands, decides that, since he has never seen the warm waters off the coast of Mexico and South America, he will take a course nearly due south. The captain, standing behind him with one eye on the compass, taking note of the decision, and immediately seeing that it will double the mileage and triple the days of the voyage, says: "It is your decision. I respect you and I permit the course."

The next flap comes from the engine room. The chief engineer, bewildered at the lack of an order from the bridge, calls up the tube. "What speed, skipper?" The answer nearly throws the whole machinery department into chaos. "You decide!"

After the same kind of conversation, the same gobbledygook about freedom and respect and concern for the real welfare of everybody, and all that jazz, the engineer, with a shrug of his shoulders, decides that the noise level in the engine room is annoying and detrimental to crew morale, so he chooses to run at one-quarter speed. On seeing this, the captain remarks: " It is your decision. I respect you and I permit the speed."

Successive donnybrooks occur in the galley over meal menus and times, in the fo'c'sle over who will stand watch and when, in the laundry over the quality of work done, and with the entire crew over the conduct of lifeboat drill.

Soon, nothing is going well and it looks as though the whole enterprise is sure to end in disaster, for no clear orders come from the bridge and every man is doing that " which is right in his own eyes." The ship is meandering almost aimlessly thousands of miles off course, at reduced speed, and every crewman feels quite free to take advantage of any situation for his own gain, only to hear the same remark from the captain, " I respect you and I permit your decision! "

But after several days have gone by, two new factors begin to appear. First, in their obvious need for some kind of order, members of the crew band together while the captain's back is turned in a sort of vigilante self-protective system in which they set up a code of house rules and secret punishments. But secondly, a few of the crew, from the able-bodied seaman to the first mate, begin to sense a genuine recognition and acceptance on the part of the captain that they have never known before. These men find themselves more able to relate to and understand their co-workers, and wish for them the same sense of value. Whereas one group is moving in the direction of organizing the permissiveness into order for protection and personal power, another group is beginning to catch on to a community of responsibly interacting persons.

The second group come to experience more and more the fact that the captain is an authentic person, as deeply involved in all the needs of life as they are, and sees the world through the porthole of humanity, specifically the sixty who are here and now. They sense a personal reference of value and find themselves wanting to please the captain in whatever they do. Because he exalts them, they want to exalt him.

The power group, unable to respond so openly and unprotectedly, become carefully rule bound in reaction, finding the naïveté and vulnerability of the captain and his supporters unrealistic, even nauseating.

And so the voyage goes on. How it ends, how the escalating conflict is resolved, and whether or not the ship completes its trip successfully remain to be seen as time goes on. It will, of course, depend entirely on how the ethic of love, as represented by those who are relation oriented, by its own strength of enriching the sensation of personhood in all it meets, can beat the defensive devices of frightened men to the finish line.

Nobody would ever really run a ship that way. Ships are supposed to make effective voyages, deliver cargo, show a profit. An open-end policy would only provide a costly stage for the acting out of relationships both good and bad, mature and immature, and for the possible emergence of a self-starting responsibility in love.

But we have to say that there is a historic suspicion that Jesus saw society as morally open-ended. His teachings were as risky and dangerous as the sea captain's policy. But then the Master always did show that he was more interested in the crew than in the voyage!

# 1

## HOW RELIGION AND MORALS GOT TOGETHER

IS IT the purpose of the church to teach people to be good? " I send my child up there to learn the difference between right and wrong, and for some reason the teaching doesn't come through. You're falling down on your real job! "

No doubt about it, the current image of institutional religion has a primary connection with behavior, with taboos beyond reconsideration, such as those having to do with sex and murder and national loyalty. If no one else is willing to take an absolute and immovable stand, certainly the church should be the one to do it!

The questions are: Is it the purpose of the church to teach people to be good? and, Is morality the measure of their faith? In spite of the fact that there is massive sentiment on the affirmative, and yards of theologians and miles of moralists who most happily see religion in that practical category, history and Holy Scripture see it somewhat differently.

Probably the first motive that drove man toward some acknowledgment of superior forces, or the supernatural, was self-protection. Men turned to their gods to have some kind of divine help to protect them in the time of battle from their enemies and in the time of famine from the ravages of natural disaster. They felt that their god, or gods, or the deities or demiurges, or whoever they were, had some particular influence over the hostile forces of life and that by making friends with these gods, or at least by appeasing them, the powers that be would in some way make life a little bit more tolerable and endurable. So every primitive religion began by trying to appease an unknown force, and a system of worship based on sacrifice, that is, buying the favor of god, was set up. It moved logically from there to a stage of trying to figure out what this god approved or disapproved about them so that they could estimate the price of buying him off. Thus far morals, or codes of behavior, are not considered on their social merit, unless certain acts seem to be required to keep god(s) happy. These acts do not necessarily have to have any apparent human values; in fact, the acts can contradict them (as in human sacrifice). Anything to keep the green light coming from the guy in the head office! If there were a tribe, for instance, who lived under a very cruel and despotic king, the god they wound up worshiping would probably be an extension of that kind of personality. As soon as they found out what kooky things it took to keep the king happy, they simply multiplied by ten and paid the price to keep the god from getting too feisty.

We cannot underestimate the importance of this transaction as a central part of all human life, both primitive and civilized. The temples of worship dominate the ruins of the past to an unbelievable degree. Man felt, from his earliest stages of organization, that the most he had to offer was none too good, and whatever god's price tag was, it came off the top! Under no consideration can this be called nobility or morality. It was sheer investment in self-preservation — what might be called large-scale payola.

Behavior — or rather, social organization — came into the picture by the back door. While the society was gathered around the altar crying for assurances of survival, or victory, or favor, the political strategists, in cahoots with the assistant high priests, were noticing that some pragmatic house rules were needed to keep the people off each other's back. The first laws that appeared had little concern for persons, or even for morality; they just kept the worshiping community from destroying itself before the irate gods got around to it. Soon the lower-echelon boys found that their words didn't go very far because there was no element of authority, and when the top brass used the high priest to make their announcements, he " put the fear of the gods into them." So morality and religion, which are really second cousins, got into the picture as identical twins.

The picture is different in the Hebrew story only because of the intense ethical sensitivity of the people themselves. A study of the Genesis narrative is revealing in the light of its chronology. The first act is creation, the establishing of a starting point in the experience of man, therefore implying movement toward an End, somewhere, sometime. This is like the laying out of a playing field in which there is every expectancy that something significant, transcending the static essence of man, is about to take place.

The story of Adam and Eve is clearly a depicting of relationships: God to man, man with himself, and the procreative relationship of man to woman. There is no immorality as such implied in the Fall; rather, and much more, the alienation of original relationships and the loss of full personhood because of it. Or, to take that statement out of pulpit patois, the Fall is the portrayal of what happens to all of us mortals when we let our self-consciousness be limited by time and space. This isn't wrong, it's just inappropriate, like using a brand-new Cadillac for a mailbox. It misses the point of being alive. But we've used this story to maintain a monstrous guilt complex instead of seeing in it the freedom to regain the lost relationship on our own.

The point is continued in the classic bit about Cain and Abel. The key phrase here is the question with which God confronts the murderer, " Where is Abel your brother? " Even with the dim distortions of centuries of an oral tradition, the point comes through that Judaism began as a relational phenomenon and that man's uniqueness, as over against animal and plant life, is only realized in the way he can recognize his brother. This is not basically a moral, that is, a behavioral, point. It is, rather, a beginning insight of the value and cosmic importance of living personalities. God did not say to Cain, "You have done wrong, you are a murderer." He said instead: "You have alienated yourself from the point of living by destroying the dignity and integrity of your brother. And so you're cursed — handicapped."

Early in the development of this called community is the superbly symbolic legend of the Tower of Babel, told in Genesis better than any medieval chronicler could ever devise. It was a project to close the gap between God and man, or between the mystery of being and the finite present. But because the men who participated were clambering all over each other to get to the seat of power and security, to become the favored, they "began to speak in different tongues." They lost communication with each other. The whole shooting match blew up because they were trying to solve the problems of life by working away from relationships toward God. Thus, early in its history, our Judeo-Christian background discovered that God cannot be worshiped at the expense of human values, and that social disorganization is the result of the sacrificing of relationships for positions of power.

It is significant that Judaism is already a worshiping community in motion before the formal law is given to it. If you're going to insist that the Ten Commandments is a statement of morality, a clear laying down of the definition of right and wrong, you will certainly have a sticky go of it. It would be nice to have a ruler with which to measure the quality of life, to know who's safely on the side of the angels and who's outside the pale of acceptable humanity. But, ancient as it may be, the Decalogue just won't do for this. It represents the accumulated insights of a community that was really beginning to catch on to what human existence in the light of Creation was all about. It is an invitation to see the direction in which God has pointed his pitifully majestic creature, giving him a sense that the movement of life is really going somewhere after all. Remember that the people of Israel were a community in transition, en route from hopelessness to promise and expectancy. Up until the Sinai scene they were traveling more *from* the Egyptian disaster than *to* the land of milk and honey. But now it came to them that the new experience had new dimensions of priorities, of safety, of belonging.

The Grand Statement begins, not with a moral restriction, but with a conceptual expansion: " I am the Lord your God, who brought you out. . . ." It doesn't even say, " You better believe it! " with the implied accusation that if you don't, you're wrong. It does say, " You shall have no other gods before me . . . ," a deucedly realistic statement to any generation, whatever its symbols. So what we mistakenly call a " moral code " really establishes at the outset an all-encompassing *relationship* within which we are invited to realize the delights of humanity. The proscription against idolatry is another way of telling us that we only hurt ourselves when we worship as God *anything* in the created universe that is, of course, less than God.

The directives concerning the Sabbath Day and the honoring of our elders for their fullness of days are also invitations into times and relationships of honor and human acceptance. It is only after the fact that integrity as such is to be found in the open honesty of relating as persons, that the commandments on stealing, killing, adultery, misrepresentation, which launch our guilt tendencies into orbit, appear. Curiously, this age-old fragment of amazing maturity ends on what we would call a psychiatric note about " coveting," an activity for which there might be no visible evidence.

However true it may be that these commandments are accompanied by the accusations of " sin," " unrighteousness," " guilt," and " wrong," it becomes evident to the Biblical scholar as the different traditions of legalism grind on and the system of sanctions becomes more complicated, that there is a dimension of meaning that rises above law and order, right and wrong. It is this element which is refined out of the crude ore of the Hebrew tradition by the prophets that becomes the core of the Christian gospel, and so becomes what Christianity really means by morality today.

But we cannot dismiss the slag from the refinery easily, for it still continues to play a large part in the confused image of church and morality. The brilliance of a light can be demonstrated from the sharpness of the shadow it casts, and the force of man's drive for self-acceptance can be seen in the intensity of his guilt feelings. Whatever the psychiatric or religious definition of guilt may be on paper, it cannot describe the monumental production every culture has made of it. Crafty leaders have found that by manipulation of guilt-provoking pressures, otherwise rational and sophisticated people can be maneuvered by the gross into the most unbelievable things. The psychopathic antics of Saul of old, Ivan the Terrible, and Rudolf Hess show this as a sickness in already sick men. Francis of Assisi, Martin Luther, and Jawaharlal Nehru were healthy men who had to shake off the infection to rise to greatness. And all of us have gone through our phases of feeling unclean even to unworthiness because of anxious guilt.

It is to the benefit of even the most legalistic of the Hebrews that direct means were sought to alleviate the poison of guilt. The classic story of the scapegoat in the wilderness is, in my humble opinion, reality *in antiquo*. But inasmuch as the custodians of the faith so early in history confused the invitation to relational worthiness given in the Decalogue with a system of ethical merit in God's eyes, the fight against guilt has been a losing battle. We raised more religious accusations of immorality provoking God's displeasure than we could supply propitiatory ceremonials to answer. That left us holding the bag, saying that we could make everything A—O.K. with God by being good little urchins without a vote in our relational decisions.

And that's how religion and morals got together. Our own

logic led us into the trap because we wanted simple systems and direct answers. The more we came to know of God, our genuine experience of his love led us to see that's the way he runs his world. So we leaped over, in our moments of self-preservation, into saying that we *ought* to be good, and if we really deliver the moral goods, God will be left without anything to accuse us of and so will have to give us some kind of prize.

The really important element that got distorted in the shuffle was the *reason* for morality. True, it is in the intimate realities of religion that any man comes to a genuine sense of responsibility for his brother, but not because he *has* to. It comes as a token of the authentic. But the ages have handed us a picture of a God who is so terribly embarrassed by our sins that he runs and hides until we have cleaned up the place a bit, and his disfavor makes us feel incomplete and sorry about the whole thing. So we try to be good, but we do it to keep him so fond of us that life goes well, and that we may even get a Sunday afternoon soda.

All of this puts the emphasis on the wrong syllable. Prophetic morality is a voluntary response. It's the way we want to live because we have come to know how God deals with us. It is that exalted sense of belonging which couldn't possibly be violated by our rebellion. Therefore, we want to reflect that same sense of being honored in honoring the people who are around us.

A farmer had three sons. They were known in the town as rather difficult behavior problems. No one could remember that they had actually broken the law or hurt anyone, but they occasionally veered close to the limits of good taste. One night the police hauled them in on a charge of being noisy, boisterous, and on the streets after curfew. The chief upbraided them, telling them what a good man their father was, how hurt he would be, what a sorry thing they had done, and that their dad ought to turn them out.

" Wait a minute," said the eldest. " You're right about everything else. Dad'll be hurt real bad. But he'll never deny us. Just you watch. He'll take us back. We belong to him."

It rather sounds like the words of the prophet:

> When Israel was a child, I loved him,
>   and out of Egypt I called my son.
> The more I called them,
>   the more they went from me;
> they kept sacrificing to the Baals,
>   and burning incense to idols.
>
> Yet it was I who taught Ephraim to walk,
>   I took them up in my arms;
>   but they did not know that I healed them.
> I led them with cords of compassion,
>   with the bands of love,
> and I became to them as one
>   who eases the yoke on their jaws,
>   and I bent down to them and fed them. . . .
>
> How can I give you up, O Ephraim!
>   How can I hand you over, O Israel! . . .
> I will not execute my fierce anger,
>   I will not again destroy Ephraim;
> for I am God and not man,
>   the Holy One in your midst,
>   and I will not come to destroy.
>
> (Hos. 11:1-4, 8a, 9.)

It's not enough to write off the connection between religion and morality that easily. So we can say it shouldn't have happened; it did happen — to such a degree, in fact, that for any religionist to say that he has no intention of being a teacher of morals is to make him look like a first-class libertine and modern heretic. And, of course, there *is* a connection, whether it is theologically or historically honest or not; it is the connection that is found in the suspicions which motivate all of us.

The history of the Christian church is an example of confusion in the bleachers that eventually reached the playing field. It cannot truly be said that Judaism was completely legalistic; in fact, it is within the high-level insights of that community that the whole relationship presuppositions of Christianity are born. But it can be said that the most widely spread self-interpretation of Judaism made a god of the Torah and equated human purity with holiness. We do not need to dwell on the elaborate, elongated detail that rabbinic writings make of the code of the law, nor on the prolonged prescriptions of devotional/moral obedience that became by Jesus' time the kosher expression of faith. His own dealings with those who criticized his Sabbathbreaking bear their own evidence of what he was up against. Enough to say that in those very conflicts is to be found the representation of exactly what religion has to expect when it proclaims relationships as the guide to morality instead of vice versa.

But no sooner was the new community of the church under way than the transmission lines were again crossed, and evidence of sincerity was sought for in proof of purity. The strongest words of Paul and some of the early fathers were directed at this problem, but by the time the church and the establishment joined forces in A.D. 325 under Constantine, institutional religion had once again become the warehouse of public morality. The behavioral tail was wagging the theological dog. It is probably one of the ironies of all time that the one community which had come into existence to proclaim the dissolution of guilt as mankind's most anxious burden was once again in the business of deliberately provoking men to feel guilty!

Soon the architects of a vast system of moral theology went to work, defining Christian obedience in terms of performance and splitting the same old hairs on what a righteous act is, measuring in figurative kilometers the distance between the sinner and an infinite God. Once this train of *non sequiturs* was started, there was nothing left but to carry it clear through to the inevitable conclusion, and the perishable hope for acceptance in a relationship of loving recognition was once again hidden in the forbidden Holy of Holies, where man cannot live and God does not relate.

The result of all this was that in historic Christian terms morality became a duty and a requirement to salvation. " You must be moral and obedient to be a Christian." There was nothing in it of volunteer response or a sense of gladness about loving because of being loved. There was, instead, the threat of the dire consequences of unfaithfulness. Authorities of the church were expected, and expected it of themselves, to be the announcers and interpreters of the difference between " right " and " wrong," these terms being used to mean what is allowed by the religious establishment as proper expressions of the law of God. The concepts of " natural law " and " divine law " were given as " orders " that were the borders of the faithful life.

To the question, " Why do you follow Christ? " the early disciples would have answered: " Because we love and trust him. In following him and leading the kind of life that would please him, we find the whole purpose of living." But to the medieval Christian or to the post-Reformation Protestant Christian, the answer to that same question might honestly be, " We have to, to save ourselves from condemnation." A second question, " Why do you lead a life of moral quality? " would have brought this from the early disciples: " We want to, to honor him whom we love, though we know he doesn't require it of us. Yet it is our privilege to witness to his love by loving others." Again, the later Christians would say: " We have to. That's what it means to be a Christian. No tickee, no washee! "

The result: the perennial pain in the ecclesiastical neck. " I just can't go to that church when I know that some of those people up there lead such unchristian lives." Or, " I just don't see what good there is in going to church when the people I know who do go aren't any better than I am." Whether or not these observations have any truth is unimportant. They probably do. Those of us in the church see far more corruption and moral failure here than the outside world has ever dreamed of. It's just that the folks who say these things miss so much of the real gladness of belonging to a community that accepts us as we are. Incidentally, they miss some pretty good gossip by staying away too!

Institutional religion has therefore pushed its adherents into much that is artificial morality, or token goodness, mainly because it felt called upon to demonstrate its validity. No doubt some of the institutionalizations, such as hospitals and schools, have produced good. But there have also been organized projects such as the holy wars, the Crusades, the witch burnings, and the Inquisitions, which have come from the same inner pressures to show faithfulness to the letter of the law. If you're going to play, you're going to play to win, and you'd better make a touchdown occasionally or you're just not with it!

This is the embarrassing position with which religion — and especially the Christian church: ecumenical, resourceful, institutionally strong, and publicly acclaimed — faces the modern day. Strong strains of theological honesty are popping up like small prairie fires among the leadership, but the majority of the constituency fears a total abdication of moral certainty and is as yet unconvinced that the church as a community is ready to follow the risky path to a relational ethic. Yet, as long as the day is put off, so long will the church (and all well-intentioned faithful people) be faced with impossible and frustrating moral predicaments for which the Christian teaching will prove irrelevant and even contradictory to conscience. The present California discussions concerning legislation permitting new criteria for therapeutic abortions are a case in point. The Roman Catholic Church, supposedly always on the side of humanity and justice, is strangled by its own quixotic moral theology, and is forced to stay on the side that has to put the letter before the spirit. Its own image is legalistic instead of relational. Protestants need not smirk; their tradition is not necessarily so wildly different.

" I sent my child up there to learn the <u>difference between right and wrong,</u> and it isn't coming through. You're failing! " We did tell him about Jesus, but the rumor went uncorroborated at home. It's not an easy point to get across.

# 2

## THE IMPOSSIBLE LUXURY
## OF VIRTUE

THERE IS no such thing as a morally defensible position. That is, to be " right " in any ethical situation is impossible. True, we have fallen into the habit of thinking there are " right " and " wrong " positions, and made ourselves feel clean about the first and guilty or inferior about the second. It's a pretty dangerous system — it's a sickness to feel guilty and, morally speaking, more sick to feel the opposite: justified, righteous, " right."

It was Jesus' sharp retort, " Why do you call me good? " when someone accused him of being good that sets the tone here. His whole ministry, directed toward loving relationships with all people, had no intention of establishing a posture of " goodness," only that which is *appropriate* in love. He knew that he moved among those who wanted the assurance that they were morally safe, and he wasn't about to give it to them. To him such an assurance would be misleading. He had no interest in heavenly or social bookkeepings, or in whose name was on what list. He related to those around him only in respect for their humanity and in sharing their creation.

When he wanted to encourage his hearers, assuring them that they were on the right track, he used the word " happy " ("blessed"), which refers to an inner self-acceptance. He never said anyone was "right," which connotes being on the safe side as far as external judgment goes. If he had given even the slightest concern to moral safety, his own life would have been considerably more restrained. He may even have stayed out of trouble.

By the standards of his day and, to be honest, most of the standards of our day, Jesus could not be called "good," or "right," or "law-abiding," or "obedient." He was none of these. He violated the Sabbath for love. He violated the dietary proprieties for love. He disturbed the public institutions for love. He refused to condemn adultery or prostitution. He even invaded the processes of nature, as seen in disease and psychopathy, by healing in love. And finally, he invaded the sacrosanct finality of death, in love.

It is ironical that the legalistic thinkers of our day look back and grant him a posthumous label of being "right" which he never sought for himself. It is startling that they do this by granting exceptions because he was unusual, yet claiming for us the necessity of being "good" to be his disciples.

Evidently, he didn't consider it much of a virtue to be found on the legal, or the safe, or the moral, or the publicly acceptable side of an issue. He was well aware that he stood in a society that was dramatically divided into the "good" and the "bad," or, as they put it then, into the "righteous" and the "sinners," ranks to be attained by external observations on behavior. "And why do you not judge for yourselves what is right?" he thundered. "As you go with your accuser before the magistrate, make an effort to settle with him on the way, lest he drag you to the judge, and the judge hand you over to the officer, and the officer put you in prison." (Luke 12:57-58.) The genuine resolution to an offense, he here maintains, is an honest interpersonal reconciliation in love. The verdict of an impersonal court will be the product of the legality of the situation, but you should be concerned with the problems of alienation and restoration first.

All of this, of course, flies in the face of our tradition, as it did in the Jewish society of his day. The danger of ever talking about standards of morality is the implication that there are " good " people who obey the law and who are therefore a more praiseworthy type of human being. And these are the ones we prefer to have in church. " I'd rather be right than President," said someone who obviously was not the President, and the medieval church felt constrained to refuse communion to those who had not been absolved of their ineligibility by becoming good via the sacrament of penance.

Why, therefore, be good? To be safe, to escape accusation and guilt, to be respected and trusted, to help make a world of social responsibility, to give every man his rightful share of justice: these are all *defensive* reasons. " I don't care what happens to me, I want to do the *right* thing." These noble-sounding words could possibly be retranslated: " Whatever the eventual justice of the situation, I want to feel morally adequate." The important part is, " I want to feel. . . ." The subjective evaluation comes topside as the real motive, and the *de facto* act of love has to be measured against the afterglow of " feel."

A high school student confesses to a certain teacher whose opinion he values that he has stolen a car, and that he knows of three other classmates who have done the same. The teacher, telling himself that " honor comes above sentiment," turns the boy in to the school authorities, saying that he couldn't live with himself if he had not done the " right " thing. It was really for the boy's welfare; the boy needed to be caught and held responsible. Whether or not the teacher did the appropriate thing is difficult for us to know, but to take him at his own word, we can say that he did it for the wrong reasons. He was thinking defensively and treating himself to the luxury of a morally justifiable memory. When the situation popped upon him, his thought was, " How can I handle this so that I have done the right thing? " A New Testament attitude would more lovingly have been, " What role can I play in these lives which upholds love and justice for them and society? "

A bus driver, far behind schedule, with his coach full of tired, homebound commuters, is upbraided by a drunken and cantankerous passenger. Block after block the man harasses the driver with obscenities and criticisms. Remembering that the drivers' manual requires courtesy at all times, the driver bites his lip and determines to endure the tirade, but his inner resentments rise rather strongly, and his driving becomes a little fast and jerky. He could stop and order the drunk off, but there would be a complaint to the company and his record affected. Besides, the other passengers want to get home P.D.Q. He is thinking defensively. The lives of the passengers would be much safer if he were to risk the snapback and put the man off, but his inner feelings tell him that it would be the " wrong " choice to make. In an ethic of love, which thinks of the most for the most, he could readily have put the man out.

One of the most clinically pure examples of defensive thinking is to be found in *some* of the reasons for pacifism. Rather than assess the immediate situation, the nearby needs for justice, it is possible for many to espouse the stand of pacifism in order to have a *clearly morally proper position*. Jesus said not only that killing was bad but that even a hostile epithet puts one in " danger of hellfire." Therefore, in time of war or threat of war, one can pull one's own self-image together by assuming an absolutely moral position. The danger of putting it even this way is the sure peril of making it appear that no pacifist acts in altruistic love, which could be one of the classically unjust statements of the century. That many choose this position in full selfless offering up of themselves on the altar of mankind is too true to allow a misunderstanding. But it is also obvious that one of the great attractions of a pacifistic point of view is its simplistic assurance of " rightness." The writer of these words speaks from inside the tepee. When I was a college student during World War II, vastly bewildered by the moral ambiguities of war and the inability of organized religion to meet the issue with any leadership, and wanting more than anything, and at any cost, to think of myself as " right," I greedily embraced the pacifistic position as that which spoke the word of sanity. In retrospect, I acknowledge that not only was I thinking defensively but I was freely giving the unfortunate implication that those who were not so morally heroic had unthinkingly sold out to the military establishment.

This is not to say that pacifism, or militarism, or any position in between or on the fringe, is superior or inferior. Any stand must be validated more by its motives than by its historical judgments. It is to say that defensive thinking about ethical decisions is not necessarily loving thinking, and leads to safety in which justice is less important than " rightness."

There are some passing poignant scenes in the Gospels in which we see Jesus dealing with defensive thinkers. The elder brother in the parable whose hero is the prodigal son brings a whole detailed paragraph to the end of that story. When he displays indignant irritation to his father about the injustice of the whole disgusting scene, pointing out that he had piled up a record of virtue quite superior to his brother's, " yet you never gave me a kid, that I might make merry with my friends" (Luke 15:29), he was voicing the hurt cry of all of us legalists: " We've been good little boys. How come the celebration, when we're the ones who ought to be the guests of honor? " The question *seems* to be a good one, until you see that there need be no other rewards given to those who think defensively; they've already received their reward in the clean feeling of being safe.

The famous scene of the paralyzed boy being let down through the roof is another opportunity Jesus used to point out the difference. When he said, " Take heart, my sons; your sins are forgiven," there was a groan of scorn from the crowd (Matt. 9:2). Jesus responded by challenging them to see whether or not he was covering his own tracks by doing something no one could question. " For which is easier [less loving], to say 'Your sins are forgiven,' or to say 'Rise and walk'? " It was evidently a much more important event in the life of the cripple, who may have been left out of the mainstream of humanity for years, to experience acceptance and renewal than to get his legs back. Jesus, seeing that which was man's greatest need, fulfilled it, not to strengthen his own prestige, but to do the loving act. Then he added the miracle of healing; however, by this time it was no longer a defensive act on his part but a proper part of his ministry to the lad.

Transpose that story into a modern scene. A certain devout man has a friend who is an alcoholic. Late one night the friend comes, weeping and in his cups, to cry out that his wife has left him and he has lost everything. " Please go to her," he sobs. " Tell her I'll do anything. I'll commit myself for treatment. I'll honestly try to stop drinking. Please, please, help me! " The defensive thing to do, to keep aboard a sense of ethical dealings, would be to bring the man in, give him hot coffee and a place to rest, thence go into the night to seek out the missing wife and deliver the message. On the other hand, the loving thing to do may more likely be to slam the door in his face and shout through the transom, " Tell her yourself! " Or it may be to go through the hot coffee bit, but turn the conversation entirely to his own self-healing — " What did you have in mind? " — and ignore the dramatic pleadings about the wife. It all depends on *whose* good the host is thinking of — his friend's or his own.

Even to say that we are continuously confronted with ethical decisions is to think defensively, for the mind then jumps to the question, " What shall I do to field this subject properly? " It immediately makes a subject out of the object; it brings attention to *me* and what I must *do*, instead of to you and how you need to be loved. Judaism had been a code of direction on how to respond to the ethical problems that the world throws at man. Jesus proposed a life that throws the love of God into every scene and creates its own moral action; it is a direction of *action* rather than of *reaction*. " Seek ye first his kingdom and his righteousness." " Be perfect even as your Father in heaven is perfect."

In the famous story of the woman taken in adultery it is

defensive thinking that is precisely the point. She was obviously guilty, and the law was clear. So the opportunists saw a way of putting Jesus on the pan, by placing before him as clear-cut a case as Jewish law provided, to see how he would weasel out. They well knew that this was exactly where his ideas and traditional "righteousness" came in on a collision course. While the gleeful crowd was assuring itself that Jesus' back was most certainly against the wall and that he most assuredly was desperately trying to figure out an escape tactic, Jesus was considering the most loving alternatives. Whatever he wrote on the ground remains a mystery, but that great Biblical student of our day, Cecil B. DeMille, suggests that he wrote the words of human sickness: " adulterer," " murderer," " thief," " liar," etc., and it stands as just about as good a guess as anyone can make. At any rate, the direction of accusation slowly rotates from the victim to the crowd itself, reassembling into a community realization. Each person present somehow began to feel himself confronted as damningly as was the woman. The warmly human closing conversation could almost be considered the catechism of Christian ethics. "Woman, where are they? Has no one condemned you?" "No one, Lord." "Neither do I condemn you; go and . . ." do your best! Wrongdoing may be harmful to society and a sickness to the doer, but guilt, when used as a poisoned-tip arrow of accusation to expiate the rest of us, is sicker.

If Jesus had been defensive, he might have gone on one of two alternate levels. First, " How can I handle this to save my reputation as a fast thinker and clever teacher? " He might have retreated into irrelevant repartee, or argued down the lawyers on their own terms of logic and law; or he might have shrugged his shoulders and said: " You've got me there. Have at it." The second, and somewhat better, level would have been: " How can I squeeze some moral teaching into this, using the unfortunate woman as a sacrificial lamb? O.K., fellows, take her and do what you must. But we're all in this together, and nobody's perfect, you know." He might then have been able to walk away reassuring himself that he had tried to do his best — it was the only right thing to do.

But the stellar fact of the matter is that Jesus wasn't a defensive thinker. He had no interest at all in either protecting his life and reputation or coming through this little hassle smelling as sweet as a rose. His fullest concern was for *all* the people involved, and how they could come through the situation honestly with their humanity intact, their self-acceptance ennobled, and the effective issues of life faced with integrity. This, probably, was one of several incidents in which hostile feelings against Jesus were stirred and collected. The fact that he showed no interest in either self-protection or martyrdom was the chief point of irritation to his opponents. Since a legalistic society is based on defending and surviving, the foolishness of anyone who gave himself so completely without providing an escape hatch was a red-alert alarm. Eventually, it became intolerable.

We cannot underestimate the significance of the outgoing ethic. The centuries had worn the sense of social responsibility smooth to the describable position of being defensive. Be good and you'll be safe. Develop a system of reaction habits to ethical situations in which your own integrity and citizenship turn up on the right side (regardless of what else happens), and you have fulfilled your Jewish, law-respecting, ethically sensitive heritage. You have obeyed God, whom to anger is to die. He is kept rather happy, distantly paternally approving, by your keeping your nose clean. How is a man to endure the day, unless he has an inner feeling that all is well with his soul and that God smiles on him? Therefore, keep the law, refrain from the big crimes, stay away from those things which bring sanction and disapproval, repeat the ceremonial formulas — this is real living!

The first thing to be seen about Jesus is that virtue is a luxury he doesn't need. His sense of self-acceptance, of inner well-being, is oriented entirely around being free from self-protection to relate in love. The people among whom he moves are the object of his adoration, and the touch of healing, the word of encouragement, the involved and expensive relationship, are his acts of worship. No law holds him back, and any law is expendable if it interferes with his being able to love. Nor does he seem to care whether his code of ethics keeps him safe, or popular, or in good standing with institutional religion, or even a hero in the eyes of the very people to whom his ministry is addressed.

It's not going to be easy for us, even after twenty centuries of mild exposure to the Jesus ethic, to deal with the fundamental motives we all have toward " decency " and " morality." These basic tendencies have to do far more with our opinion of ourselves, and the equipment of useful prefabricated responses to standard situations, than with channels of loving. We also have to admit that the majority power of Christian tradition has taught us to think defensively. We are supposed to confess Christ as our Lord *and Savior*. We are supposed to live moral lives so that we are assured of a *heavenly reward*, or, to put that in the context of the social gospel, so that we may have the assurance of a clean conscience. We desperately look around for those symbolic actions of goodness, like the Boy Scout's daily good deed, which will protect the corrosion of the self-image. Our own history has taught us to be idolaters, and an externally correct morality is our idol.

But Jesus does not condemn us in our idolatry, nor does he bring the " wrath of God " down upon our heads because we have missed the point of our own humanity. Rather, he shares our predicament with us and only levels the finger of accusation where we have already leveled it at ourselves. In this respect, the parable of Lazarus and the rich man (Luke 16:19-31) is a glistening jewel. The plot opens with a scene that everyone would formally agree contains elements of injustice: a man with everything who lives it up and cares for no one, and a man who has nothing but disease and poverty. The former calls for help, and Jesus, the teller of the story, shows that the man neither gets it nor deserves it. It just goes to show you, say the hearers, there is an eventual justice after all, and that old fellow is getting the torment he deserves.

But the story stoppeth not there. The rich man becomes a little less villainous, for his thoughts turn to the needs of others. "Send him to my father's house, for I have five brothers, so that he may warn them, lest they also come into this place of torment." And in tender sadness, Father Abraham has to tell him that there is no way to break through to the defensive thinker, unless he himself wants to love. Here Jesus does not avoid the reality of nonloving and its damaging consequences, nor the hard facts that even love is limited by the privacy of those who reject it. But somehow as we hear this story, we realize that we have been exposed without being accused. We sense the shabbiness of defensive thinking and realize in the privacy of our hearts our own alienation from "Father Abraham." Yet no one has clobbered us with an ego-destroying condemnation. Our own self-condemnation has been far more withering, far more redeeming.

And all this time we really wanted to be virtuous. In a society of ethics as a way to acceptance, we wanted more to be accepted at any price than to understand the investment of accepting. We honestly *do* love people, want the best for them, and freely give hours and ergs and gallons of our life and love to the service of others. As a matter of fact, we just couldn't stand the possibility that we might *not* be loving. Promise me anything, but let me believe I'm human, and loving, and a good guy, and appreciated for my niceness. The pious credos of the American service clubs are institutionalized headstones of this syndrome: "Service Above Self," "Service to Mankind," "We Help Others." If one tilts his head a little to one side, he can almost hear the blast of the trumpets over the alms box, a humorous editorial cartoon that Jesus once drew with biting tongue.

It's always easy to sit in judgment on history. But there is a certain trend in diplomatic relations that appears to be international defensiveness. Chamberlain returned from Munich to proclaim "peace in our time." All he had really done was to protect the British image from the label of "aggressor," which has the same moral tone in national affairs as " adulterer " or even " pervert " has in the personal sphere. The intransigence of nations to act selflessly when the prairie fires of insurgence, conspiracy, or famine break out is massive defensiveness. Probably one of the most fortunate, guilt-alleviating, defensiveness-preserving turns of international good luck in the twentieth century was the Japanese attack on Pearl Harbor, which permitted the American entry into the war with heroic, spotless, knight-errant flags aflying. Heaven only knows what manipulation would have been necessary if the Japanese military had not so clearly handed us our own passport to purity in a white envelope!

I well remember sitting in the gallery of the United Nations Security Council in November of 1965, watching the heated discussions on the problem of Rhodesia. This mid-African, white-dominated country had just severed relations with the United Kingdom so it could continue suppression of the black majority. Britain lamented the whole nasty mess and, supported by the United States, was trying to save face by saying so without intervention. His Excellency Alex Quaison-Sackey of Ghana, representing the African bloc, protested in biting oratory that Britain was all words and no action. " It just goes to show that if a white man's head is on the block, the British lion will roar and strike. But if the lives of only a million blacks are at stake, it will only whimper and lick its paws." There just wasn't a fortunately clear-cut, dramatic token of righteousness to get the lion off his haunches.

At this writing, the ambiguity of the " cause " in Vietnam has vitiated the enthusiasm of America for our presence there. It is a caustic comment to make that if only there had been some kind of atrocity (or even a clear, hostile threat from the lips of Ho Chi Minh), the United States would be able to have a clearer national conscience. We simply have to have a moral justification, dumped on us by some outsider, so that we are not in danger of feeling uneasy about what we are doing. It is very probable that one major atrocious incident, or a demonic proclamation from Peking itself, wouldn't alter the real issues one whit, but it would make us feel better about it.

This reveals the hypocrisy that always has to be promoted within nations at war because of the defensive idea that war is caused by, or settles, moral issues. Administrations have to whip up a warlike frenzy among their peoples on the basis that war is " right." Thank God for Irving Berlin and his music! Practically no one says that war is at this time and in this place a practical strategy. That sounds too cold, and besides, you can't get boys into the front lines with the same argument you'd use to get them to clean fish. So Pope Urban II sprang the first Crusade into life with the cry, " God wills it." W. R. Hearst bled so much about the nasty Spaniards that even Teddy Roosevelt went charging up San Juan Hill (Bully!), and World War I was lubricated by some of the most gruesome atrocity stories ever invented.

The reason we have arrived at this rather dishonest method of intranational conversation is that we have fostered defensive morality. To settle our " conscience " in reaction to unpredictable problems we have to have a " reason." This has to have all the aspects of justifiable homicide, or we will be so overcome with guilt as to feel unclean, and that would be downright inconvenient. Besides, nations have to put forth that kind of special effort in wartime which only a near-religious zeal can produce. And how do you stir up this zeal? You guessed it.

Virtue is a defensive word. If we want to be virtuous, we are asking for a special place in the universe that the realities of this world just don't offer. " Why do you call me good? There is none good but God." " There is none righteous, no, not one." The whole question of morality immediately becomes clouded by virtue. Just do what you can, and love without self-consciousness of it. And let virtue be damned!

# 3

---

## MORALITY *AD HOMINEM*

*AD HOMINEM* is a Latin phrase meaning "toward man." It is used to describe a line of thought or action that uses the present situation of man as its reference point. Jesus had an *ad hominem* ministry in that it was always pointed in the direction of men, whom he seemed to understand. It therefore appears rather sensible to think of "morality" in terms of looking at man, seeing both the "is" and the "ought" and adjusting our relations accordingly.

When one looks at the life of Jesus one sees rather strikingly that Jesus is so very mobile, on the move, carrying his outwardly directed concern to people. The Oriental idea of the holy man may see him in pilgrimage to some shrine, or lying on his couch propped up on one elbow, receiving those who came seeking advice. Not so with Jesus, to whom the world was one great vacuum into which he was drawn because of his active love for the people in it. He deliberately sought out the arenas of life and life's infections, and moved toward the different situations where people sang their songs, licked their wounds, worshiped their gods, fought out their resentments. Though it is true that in doing this he put himself in places where what he represented had to go on trial, yet the flow of affection and interpersonal care started in him and surged outward without interruption.

Another of his commanding characteristics is that he caused his own moral decisions. Whatever took place between Jesus and any person or group that confronted him was mostly on his terms, and the subject was always immovably the personhood of those involved. It is quite true, as T. W. Manson tells us, that Jesus realized he had three audiences and behaved somewhat differently to each, namely, the public, the enemies, and the inner circle of followers. The behavior was, indeed, different, but the subject matter was the same: the humanity of his hearers and their heritage as reflections of God.

Look at the bookends of his relationships with each of these three. He began his leadership with the disciples in an invitation, " Come, follow me." He ended it by saying, " Go, make learners. . . ." With the multitudes he started with a list of happinesses; he ended by cleaning the entrenched economic exploiters out of the Temple so that it could be a " house of prayer for all peoples." To his enemies he carried the battle of aggressive love in a chiding fraternization, and ended by praying for their forgiveness. Wherever he was, there was the atmosphere of an unapologetic, person-oriented, thoroughly loving morality.

We learn so much about ourselves by seeing how others treat us. Especially do we learn, and willingly respond, under the tender ministrations of someone we can trust, someone who is evidently fond of us. That's why we can see so much about ourselves in the manward respect that was such a powerful part of the life of Jesus.

On a recent trip, we left our native country on two occasions, once to go into Canada and then into Mexico. Though we went to see the places we visited, we were impressed by the most unexpected added reward of a backward look at our own land from the outsider's perspective. It is one thing to discuss America with Americans; it is quite a different experience to stand on foreign soil and talk about the world's richest people from without.

In a view of man-directed morality, it does us little good to discuss what we need from inside the camp. We have to assume that Jesus saw us from a vantage point we don't usually occupy — his reactions to our good and bad, our accomplishments and failures, were surprisingly different from what we expected. What *did* he see? Why was he not more shocked and less loving? Of course, we cannot really be objective about ourselves, but we ought to try.

Evidently we humans have a small list of fundamental needs whose fulfillment comprises the nature of staying alive. Like a sturdy, oaken dining room table with four big thick legs, we gain the whole stability of existence from standing on and ceremonializing these four profound supports: eating, mating, socializing, and worshiping. Then, like that apparently unnecessary fifth leg which frequently was found right in the center of such a table, there is the fifth function: work.

And, to carry the picture of the table one more notch, it was quite evident that it was about the most solid piece of furniture in the whole house. Yet if one of the four peripheral legs was missing, or broken, or uneven, the whole table was unsteady. As a matter of fact, even with five substantial legs, if only one of the corners was unsupported, a whole half of the surface was insecure, and the whole table could be tipped by the pressure of one mischievous finger, sending dishes and precious bric-a-brac cascading to the floor.

Don't ask me to explain it. The complexities of the human situation and the uncertainties as to the components of a wholesome life are beyond my limited ability to reason. But we do have to describe our world in coming to know how to function in it, and this table illustration is a way of describing what many generations of human experience tell us about man, and what Jesus must have seen in us to do as he did. I don't understand the alimentary canal, especially the intricacies of the organic chemicals secreted by the proper glands and all that. But, from a layman's point of view, I think it necessary to have a working description of the process so that I know what to do about, or at least what importance to attribute to, a stomachache or an onset of gas. If we don't know how to interpret the signals of our biggest needs, we have a rougher time of life than we need to.

So we have the four legs of the table: not just the raw, unadorned, simple functions of eating, mating, etc., but each surrounded by a whole host of traditions, meanings, myths, legends, and especially rituals. Life *could* be sustained if we all ate from a common dispensary, clapping full hand to mouth en route to other tasks, but we don't do it that way. The institutionalizing of eating has been of first-rate importance since the first burp. Perhaps it all began with the experience of feeding at mother's breast, when the infant was fuzzily aware that along with the filling of the stomach was the filling of something else far less tangible but just as important — the living sensation of a relationship of dependence and security. Possibly this was continued as the family gathered around a new kill or a centrally cooked meal and sensed that there was a relatedness about the family which checked in for value somewhere above the stomach. At any rate, eating per se is now just the central activity around which a meal or a gathering, feast, celebration, date, business conference, or restful chitchat nearly always occurs.

We eat to stay alive. It's a fundamental drive; our bodies just have to have nourishment and calories and vitamins and carbohydrates and all that. But eating is far more important than the ingestion of fuel for the biological furnace. It is a ritualistic expression of our humanness, our relatedness, our cultic forms, our selfhood. No person alive is devoid of atmospheric enrichment of his meal, even though it is the roving eye of the solitary truck driver in the all-night hash house following the curvaceous waitress to the coffee urn. And everyone looks forward to his high festivals: the family Thanksgiving dinner, the romantic dinner by candlelight with wine, the testimonial retirement dinner, the church potluck supper, and on and on. We are so accustomed to eating's being in some context of ceremonial assurance that eating alone or without grace or napkin is empty indeed, even though it organically fills the bill.

To say that man must eat is a dull obviosity. Of course he must. But to say that eating is necessary to life is an understatement. We eat, but in the process we do more than eat. We minister not only to our stomachs but to our morale, our cultus, our sociality, our sense of selfness and humanity, and we wouldn't think of reducing meals to mere eating. Life is more than that. To the necessity of eating we have added the joy of being people who are alive, who can ascend to aesthetic dimensions of eating and other trappings.

The solidity of this leg is found not in its bare necessity but in what it adds to the experience of being, in doing the things that enable us to be. Animals eat, but people eat and relate. The ritualness of it all helps us describe to ourselves what we are, or can be, or ought to be, and we enrich it with the legends of eatingness.

Another leg of this table is mating, the whole cycle from courtship to domestic establishment. This too has its organic biological core, but what an aura of ritual! From the Song of Solomon to Elizabeth Taylor, from the removal of the first fig leaf to the marriage of your oldest daughter, this area has been described most completely in sixty-six percent of all literature written, and in ninety-two percent of all songs sung through the centuries. We mate to perpetuate the race, but, merciful heavens, what a production we have made of it! And it wasn't some stuffy philosopher poring over his books in a dusty castle who imposed this whole thing on us, either! We did it all ourselves, yessirree, with a lot more to come, as long as humanity is created in two genders. Does anyone in the back row care to protest that life would be just as much fun without mating? or with mating, but without all the mythology, background music, flirtation, and perfume? It's all part of the human scene, brother, and you might as well know it. Need we say more?

The socializing of meaningful acts is the bouncing of our personalities against others to get identity and reference. Just as the tumbling machine of the rock hound turns and turns and turns and polishes nondescript-looking stones into near-gems, so the activity of personal relationships forms us into what we are. The structures of social, political, and religious life, complicated and profound as they are, all begin with the inner compulsion to relate to others. Here we find our channels of expression for hostility and love, for service and greed, for friendship and mutuality. Here too is ritualization and organization, in Masonic Lodge, Rotary, friendship " cliques," neighborhood coffee klatches, dates, Ku Klux Klan rallies, and cocktail parties. Apparently, these are fluffy nonessentials which we all say we could get along without, but we never do. No community anywhere on earth went into its second day of existence without elaborately contrived group relationships. We can only conclude that these relationships are essential to life.

So we come to the fourth leg, which is the real point of the whole illustration. Man just has to worship. No culture whose footsteps yet remain in history has ever tried to exist without worship, and most cultures have made this the most elaborate of all functions. From the majestic ruins of the Acropolis in Athens, to the silent remains of Chichén Itzá in Yucatán, and back to the pyramids of the Nile, the architecture of all times is pointed to something beyond visible man. Cause and effect studies such as the observations of Toynbee show that religious aspirations have shaped and clarified the values of any culture, bringing moral sensitivity on an upward path until overtaken by a curious, introverted decay that always seems to be prefaced by religious deterioration.

So, starting with the evidences of history and peering at the steeples and temples that clutter the horizons of cities ancient and modern, we have to say that men have always given considerable importance to worship. If we wanted to compound the evidence even more by assembling detailed factual information, we would discover that a large proportion of any generation's economy has gone to religious expression. If you want to know what a person's real loyalties are, look at the stubs in his checkbook, I always say. Further, the best in buildings, the most excruciating of physical effort, the most time-consuming of pursuits, and the most inclusive subject in literature, all seem to involve religion. People don't piddle around with non-essentials on levels like that.

Take the subject of human emotions. Fear, guilt, love, hatred, adoration, are all involved in different aspects of the four fundamental legs, but come to their most profound exploration and expression in religious ideas or rituals. The advanced cultures had advanced religions in which the dynamics of emotional release were rather delicately spelled out. The Holy Roller of today is simply a modern King David dancing out his victory feeling before the high altar, and the well-disciplined choir at Riverside Church is continuing the fertility chants of the South Pacific Maoris. It becomes abundantly clear that where there is no organized religious outlet for corporate feelings, the community either creates one or ceases to be a community.

So we have to believe. At least, every man who has preceded us has had to, and he left his diary for us in the form of some rather phenomenal traditions. True, one could say that all this evidence looks backward into the past, and we are talking about the characteristics of ancient man, no longer a fact of life. We could point out that the office-building skyscrapers of New York have long since towered over Trinity Church, and that modern life has nowhere near the architectural evidence of religious prominence that the past has, and that things have changed. Modern man, we can say (and many of us do), is so sophisticated that he has caught up with himself and no longer needs the superstitious folderol to keep his spirits up that his fathers did. He has punctured the mystery of space, delved into the nature of matter, found he could manipulate the organic dimensions of life, and released the power of the atom. Also, ethics has largely become a matter of having considerable room to do what you can get away with, without too severe sanctions. The sense of awe can be satiated by stereophonic music, panoramic multicolored movies, stupendously high buildings, and clever planetariums. The fear of the holy can be imitated by an afternoon of water-skiing, or driving lickety-split down a crowded freeway, or going to a drag race, or betting your life savings at a crap table. Why do we need religion?

This would all be a rather convincing line of thought if it weren't contradicted by our own pathetic attempts to fill the gaps with somewhat shabby substitutes for religion. We are creatures prepared to adore, and when the *mysterium* of adoration is deflated, we turn the full force of our adoring on any nearby idol, whether or not it has feet of clay. This is seen in our use of vocabulary, how we have almost completely worn out and deflated superlative words because we directed them in inferior directions. " Colossal," " stupendous," " magnificent," " awe-inspiring," " captivated," in former times reserved for the singular moments of the Holy, excite very little response because their contexts are usually banal. As a matter of fact, contemporary English probably doesn't have any usable superlatives anymore, not because we have downgraded the divine, but because we have made the ordinary to look like the divine in our loneliness.

Let's rerun that. The psalmist maintained that he meditated on the divine law both day and night. He thought about it all day, and when he lay down, he reveled in the fact that God was, and therefore life had meaning. What puts the twinkle in modern man's eye? What puts living color into his daydreams? When you have the answer to that, you have identified either his religion or his substitute for religion, for you have nailed down his basic motivations and loyalties.

Of course, answering this question will take us into the area of conjecture, but there certainly ought to be agreement on a few generalities. Modern man dreams about the acquisition of security, goods, and recognition. He dreams about sex. He dreams about participation in sports, or hobbies, or projects, or causes. And some, probably a minority, dream about a society of justice and honor. So far we have talked about the reasonably healthy and wholesome of our contemporaries; the less so will dream in terms of power, revenge, miraculous escape, racial or sectional superiority, or the Walter Mitty megalomania.

All of these are mainly inventions to fill the vacuum, simply because our ability to long for and give loyalty to is purer than the objects of our longing and loyalty. Do we not all sense some element of sarcasm in the obvious insincerity of a TV commercial? The prospect of a housewife witnessing to her faith with evangelistic fervor, gushing over a plastic bottle of floor wax, comes across to all of us as a tolerable artificiality. We sneer at the idea that profound salvation can be found in the use of a breath sweetener, or that a woman will have found the whole purpose to life in a hair dye; yet, even as we sneer, we wonder down deep if it might not be so, and the product sells like hot cakes. The record not only goes to support the theory of successful advertising, which it does, but it also reveals the burning appetite that we all have to go hog-wild with enthusiasm over *something* — anything! If God is dead, or dull, even a mouthwash has something to offer.

We are, as a matter of fact, a culture that simply tingles with motivation to adore. Perhaps it is the advanced physical health brought on by vitamins and antibiotics, or the ennui that overtakes us because so much of life's effort is absorbed by machines. At any rate, we are more ready to devote the sharp edge of love and commitment to a genuine call to ministry than our forefathers could be. Our trouble is that our souls are all dressed up and have nowhere to go, so we piddle around the living room waiting for the great push, and get overexcited about the furniture.

Let's take those dreams again. The first was acquisition which happens to have a noble and respectable tradition behind it. Our Puritan fathers firmly believed that loyalty and obedience were the components of righteousness, and that God rewarded this kind of consistent responsibility with visible approval, namely, wealth. This subtle distortion of the gospel, by the third generation, had crept into the psyche of the Protestant culture to the extent that it was the mark of goodness to be productive. The deep abiding sense of guilt, which could not be alleviated in the nonexistent confessional booth, had to be worked out in a compulsive pursuit of this world's goods. It is no accident that the first capitalistic tycoons, the captains of industry and benefactors of much that is American, rose to their wealthy prominence on a Bible-reading, adage-quoting, self-imposed discipline that included scorn for sloth and admiration for Horatio Alger and his ilk. It became an implicit credo of Anglo-Saxon life that to be righteous meant to be rich, and that God just couldn't hold back his admiration and blessings from the clever businessman. This is one reason why slavery remained a fact of life in America long after other countries abandoned it; it was a way to make the land prosper economically and exalt the prestigious advantages of the Christian white man, and, of course, God would simply have to be for that!

So, when our brothers today do their daydreaming in terms of a bigger house, a better wardrobe, a more powerful car, and a well-planned savings and pension program, they are really kneeling in high worship. First, they are seeking to develop concrete and demonstrable evidences of an existential righteousness which will show that they have been forgiven, or, in today's terms, that their unidentifiable anxieties about existence and social responsibility can really be dissolved by proving that they have done in this world what they have been called to do. By being acquisitive, one feels more accepted in an acquisitive society; it's like scoring in a ball game on a team that's supposed to score. Everybody likes you for that, and you feel real good. The nice, comfortable, slightly ostentatious house in the slightly *exclusive* neighborhood (the word is actually used in much real estate advertising) is an indication of goodness, righteousness, the fulfilling of purpose, and the skillful catching on to what life is all about. There is a slight philosophical difficulty here as to whether or not this really fills the bill, but the anxiety is dissipated; it seems unlikely.

We also said that modern man dreams of sex, or something like that. We have already commented on the elaborate fantasies that surround this subject. It is time to ask what they mean. The fact that anyone who wants to use the symbols of sex can get a devoted following is a phenomenon in itself. It may all have started, in our day at least, when the innocuous painting of a scantily clad maiden, called *September Morn*, drew crowds and crowds and crowds, and then comments, criticisms, and cheers. For our prim pre-World War I society it came as somewhat of a shock to discover that everybody from hoboes to preachers, from schoolgirls to *grandes dames*, from the Bowery to the Bronx, wanted to see that picture and militantly chose up sides for or against it. Clever advertisers caught the implications immediately, and ever since, a large portion of our economy has been lubricated by cheesecake. Then the entertainment industry, a little bewildered because it thought it had used the gimmick before, gave cheesecake another go, and Hollywood became more important in the lives of men than the League of Nations. Jean Harlow and Marilyn Monroe have become the vestal nonvirgins sacrificed on the high altar of this faith, and each year's Miss America or Miss Universe becomes the next candidate. *Playboy* magazine, which runs articles of exceptionally high value, pays its bills because of its center-page foldout, not its literary quality, and the comparative sizes of female mammary glands occupy more time in Washington than the gross national product.

Actually, of course, the subject is not sex in its usual biological sense. The whole campaign centers around the recreational implications of a part of the subject of sex. Any mention of the responsible relation of marriage, or the long-range involvement of parenthood, would quickly throw cold water on the whole allure. Modern man isn't *that* interested in sex. He is sharply motivated by the fantasy, whether or not it ever becomes real, of the brief drama of nonresponsible mating, the chase and the conquest, the attraction and the tease, the tension and the release. But down beneath all this is the suggestion that the sex act itself always involves exposure, and at a time of vulnerability, acceptance, and mutual service. Further, the sex act is biologically exclusive, always involving two and only two persons. This suggests high pleasure, intimacy, exposure, understanding, and acceptance, in a situation where the prying, disapproving, critical, and accusing outside world is shut out. In the sex act, especially outside the involvements of marriage, every man is a king and every woman, no matter how unlovely and unattractive she may be elsewhere, is a queen for a day. There is no competition, no judgment, only (so goes the dream) high joy. So the very deepest needs of our nature, beyond the sensuous, the sexual, and the moral, are touched by the possibility of an assignation, or the dream of one. A man who, at the stimulation of current literature and image, indulges in the fantasy of disrobing a pretty woman, or a woman who longs to be seduced, is also thinking of trusting and being trusted, of expressing acceptance and being accepted, of revealing earthiness and being understood, of being adequate to the occasion and stimulating an appreciative response. These are, in themselves, amoral motives.

Our overenthusiasm for the symbolism of sex (displayed even in our adamant disapproval and scorn of the whole area) is far more a religious problem than a moral, or social, or cultural one. We have simply given witness to our capacity to adore the mysterious and to the great cost we are willing to pay for the privilege. One might even go so far as to say that the sex cultus is an affirmation of the faith cry, and needs more to be rightly interpreted as a positive thrust of the collective human spirit than to be lamented as a corrosion.

Again, man dreams about participation in causes of worth or evident accomplishment. That small fringe who are circumstantially free enough to stand up and be counted are considered extremists and oddballs, not only because they really are but because the inert majority can only look upon them with ill-concealed envy. The bearded and unwashed who enter gleefully into demonstrations for freedom of speech and expression, who protest war and racial injustice, who enrich the resources of art and literature with uninhibited soul shakers, are kissing

cousins to the John Birch Society members, the Ku Klux Kon-
nivers, and the retired businessman who walks along the Long
Beach boardwalk in purple shorts and a striped straw sombrero.
Once again, the residuum of unrelieved guilt for tolerating life
as being fulfilled essentially in the morally shadowy marketplace
makes the average American ache to see himself in some context
of selflessness, purity, and virtue. He doesn't especially want to
*be* the exemplar of righteousness. He just wants to get one reassuring glimpse of himself as *possibly* being good, and that's
why he has the strong compulsion to " forsake the temptations
of this world " and go on a pilgrimage. Who knows how much
of the money given to churches, or to elaborate foundations, or
to a plethora of charities, is pried loose from its source as a
down payment toward the purchase of a tolerable self-image?

Modern man longs to see himself as socially valuable, and
the obsession may at times exceed his search for material security. Anyone who is clever, manipulative, persuasive, and articulate can get a following and adequate financing if he trumpets his cause as noble. In point of fact, such leaders, though
they be charlatans, may be doing their disciples much good by
offering channels of participation. An impure noise that sounds
the call to humanity in dissonant tones may be better than the
silence of no cause at all.

Underneath it all is the uneasy desire to give, to expend, to
sacrifice, to deal with the gifts of life in some royal and irra-
tional extravagance. This may be the greatest danger to a
mounting stockpile of weaponry, the feeling that " it's meant
to be used — what a shame to let it go with purpose unful-
filled." Just as it is the current spirit to look upon the unused
cannon or unexploded bomb with a certain measure of sadness, so do we look upon ourselves at times with remorse. The
schoolboy who can take forty-five minutes on his way home
from school to play sandlot football and can check in at supper-
time with his clothes dirty and torn, his elbows scratched and
bleeding, his body tired and hurting all over, can also shout as
he slams the front door, " Boy, did I have fun! " He has been

able to do what his elders would fain be able to do daily. We are all microcosmic Nathan Hales, wishing we had more than one "life" to give to our "country" (or whatever), except that we spend most of our time trying to figure out how we can give whatever it is that we have without risk. Since we are really trying to find out how to fly above the clouds with both feet on the ground, the collective result and mood of the times is monumental frustration.

This dream, too, is neither a gloomy evidence of a morbid deadlock on the downslope nor a commentary on a hapless culture, but, rather, another indication that there is more to being than wishing things were different. We live with inner voices and forces that, given an honest hearing, could make us more honest with ourselves — which happens to be one of our most profound longings.

We earlier said that when we have identified man's dreams we have found his religion. So where are we? The dreams all seem to have something to do with man and superman. They parade before us the possibilities of being capable and potent, financially, sexually, morally. In our secret closets we dream dreams and see visions of a realm, a kingdom, a being, in which all the things that are true in our earthy and sensuous world are still true, but even more so. We take the dimensions of experiences that seem to ennoble us and elongate them into infinity, hoping to see parallel lines touch. We are able to make sense out of today only by working backward into it from what it might mean to tomorrow, for yesterday must remain an unsolved enigma. In other words, our dreams all point to the direction of the completion, somewhere, somehow, of what is here and now incomplete.

This is not quite the philosophical gobbledygook that it may appear to be. The business executive who lays out plans for the expansion of his industrial plant justifies the effort not only on the basis of increased profits but on the "larger benefits to the community" of increased employment and commercial growth. He is both an economic realist and an idealistic eschatologist — meaning that he talks to himself in terms of "larger goods" as though he had to persuade himself that the profit motive itself is vulgar in its nakedness. His own need for the rationale is a cry for an assurance of ultimate worth. Elijah of old may have voiced the agony of the American Rotarian when his anxiety compelled him to bemoan the fact that " I am no better than my fathers." At least men in both widely separated centuries dreamed that they ought to be.

O.K. already, so this line of thought is a little too drippy. After all, how about the " realism " of the nonconformists, the " beat " crowd who make a production of not making a production of good, or morality, or hope, or Valhalla? Is there not an admirable honesty in giving way to cynicism and despair, and in not pretending anymore that this is a moral universe? Besides, the gasser of the decade has thrown up the *ne plus ultra* of all: " God is dead! " Good point, that.

It would be a good point, that is, if, with the introduction of the bearded element as contrasted to the gray-flannel-suit crowd, we have produced a new and different argument about those dreams. But lo! When injustices real or imagined blight the land, who is on the placard line pressuring for a better order of things? Who provides the live bodies for the mass demonstrations for peace, against narrow patriotism, for freedom of speech, and against all the tiresome niceties of the *status quo?* You're ding-danged right on the first guess! Shaved or not, bathed or not, whether or not they can pluck a seven-stringed guitar, all men dream somewhat the same dreams — we just have more colorful ways of " in "-ing our hibitions.

But Nietzsche, Hamilton, Altizer, and those other noisy iconoclasts are still claiming that God is dead. How about that? Of course he is. And he ought to be — he just isn't up to the twentieth-century requirement for divine competency. He still smells of the mustiness of Inquisition cellars, of Middle-Western folk hymns, of oppressively somber Gothic and Bible-belt culturation, and he gasped his last when the world came of age.

All men have longed for God — an ultimate and absolute purity, an unwavering eternal simplicity. We have longed for him so hard that the wishful thinking has projected itself on the sky over our heads. What was blown up in the image was an accumulation of man's dreams, and not always the best ones. Nevertheless, in the projection, in the frantic struggle, it seems as though we caught a passing glint of genuine splendor, and our pulse quickened in faith and fear. It was like looking through a keyhole at a transient dream, but it was Something, and we found, because of it, that looking in a mirror wasn't all terror.

But in the twentieth century a keyhole-size God isn't enough. We have mushroom clouds and hosts advancing to the fray, impelled by hunger and hostility. Let's kill Him off quickly so that Creation and Existence don't have to be bastards. There is still time to make an " honest woman " out of the juices of life. So let God die. It seems a good line, anyway.

We started on the " dream " kick by saying that all men have a built-in need to adore. That this need sometimes comes through in negation and scorn and the obscenities hurled by " angry young men " only illustrates the fact that a sweater turned inside out is still a sweater, though not quite so tidy-looking. We still wind up with mankind all dressed up to worship and, if unbelieving, with nowhere to go. Frustrated and bitter, he falls upon his neighbor's neck in a futile, treadmill re-enactment of the Cain and Abel syndrome.

Such is the arena of confused, curiously obsessed humanity to which Jesus came. What are the ground rules of a morality that ministers in this maelstrom with love? It is quite impossible to describe any part of Christian ethics apart from the volatile possibilities of what happens when a man is confronted by someone who understands him.

It's almost begging the question to pose an ethical problem and ask, " What shall I do? " for Jesus never saw morality in that way. He saw to it that every emergent relationship was already established on his terms of a preexistent illumination of the reverence for the person in front of him. So, when the rich young man came to ask, " What shall I do to be saved? " Jesus could gently let him off the hook by allowing him to come to his own conclusion about whether he really wanted to be saved. And his decision, apparently an inferior one, was given respect by the Master. He refuses to invade the privacy of those who choose not to love.

This is the crown jewel of the way Jesus loves persons: unconditional concern. He never stipulates that a person has to perform to get the prize; he never heals for pay; nor does he withhold his love from the ungrateful. Although it is true that he asks some, " Do you really believe? " and others to retain their own dignity by performing some cooperative act like washing in the well, he leaves all doors open. There is no record that he refused to meet a genuine human need, even that of the woman who touched his garb in the crowd. Even though Zacchaeus had an inferiority feeling because of his height, and probably a grinding paranoia because of his unpopular profession, he received the same critical cleansing in honesty that the helpless leper or Simon the Pharisee did. Nor did Jesus stipulate that one had to be dutifully appreciative to make the healing valid. His only comment on this, when nine out of ten healed lepers didn't turn up to shake his hand, was a simple encouragement of the one who did. The others stayed well.

This moves the whole field of being good out of the realm of reciprocal ethics. " It is good," says one father to his sons, " to live in a society where other good people live. You can live out your days in honorable friendships, and your children can grow in safety." If this is a front-porch, post-burp observation to start the talk going, it may be acceptable. But if it is a patriarchal declaration of the reason for a moral society, it veers close to being dangerous. Love, to Jesus, was not the sense of glowing and being glowed, of liking and enjoying being liked, of serving and expecting a certain amount of courteous service in return. To him the central purpose of life was to turn on the lights of inner experience and participate in the love in which humanity is called to bask. He would have been the same if every person he met had rejected him; his healing would just have to have been more subtle. To be any different would have done such violence to his nature as to have destroyed him.

This is the essence of a manward morality, an *ad hominem* love. He understood the multifarious, the demonic, the need to adore, and the bitterness. And he loved. He didn't even have a code of morals, or a prescribed system of ethics. He moved toward people. He set the tone of morality on the basis of respect for persons, and he asked no display of worthiness.

Behold the predicament of a well-meaning Christian who wants to take some significant part in doing away with the evil of racial discrimination. He knows that the " system " is wrong, that it is grievous to think he lives in a society in which some people do not have the available breathing space to sense their own dignity. His own living arena does not give opportunities for authentic personal relationships with minority peoples. So he has to deal in abstract principles and take part in do-good organizations. When the call comes for a dramatic demonstration (such as the march from Selma to Montgomery), he either goes and grovels in the mud or stays home and wishes he had gone. He wants to protest, but his protest is mostly against his own ineffectiveness, and he wants to be able to cite certain redemptive experiences.

There is nothing amiss in his going to Alabama; it has many laudable possibilities. But if his going or not going is to him a symbol of a major coup in fighting the race war, he has been seduced into defensive thinking. His ministry is where he is, and his loving will constrain him to do many things. He could organize his own demonstrations in his office or his community, but none of them would be an assurance to him that he was morally safe; they would just be sincere expressions of a reverence for man. Whether or not his loving breaks out into big doings, his sense of appreciation and gratitude for those around him is all-important.

Morality, in Christian terms, is being specific in the areas in which the Torah could only be general. It is carrying toward the identified person the justice that the law could only say impersonally. Fletcher is quite right in saying that love and justice are the same, always. And because law at its best can only be general, morality at its best uses law as a substantial suggestion, but never as the final word. As a matter of fact, in most situations laws can militate against each other, can even conflict — such as laws for the preservation of the Sabbath working against the laws of helping disabled oxen. It then becomes left up to a standard of priority values for the legalist to make his choice. But for the Jesus ethicist, law at its best only contributes guideline suggestions which bear the value of experience but are not directives for the immediate problem. The insight, then, is the contribution of love, and is the deciding and authoritative factor. There is no evidence at all that Jesus apologized for violating the Sabbath when he healed the boy born blind (John, ch. 9). The fact is that he had not the slightest indication of a feeling of guilt or wrongdoing. He had, indeed, broken the law, but he had expressed a healing love that is, in fact, the true intent of the law.

Herewith lies the kink. Christian morality is *only* to do the loving thing manward. There are no absolutes, no unbreakable ground rules, no qualifying principles. Jesus was aggressive, active, outgoing, but these are only descriptive; above all, he was loving, which means healing, reconciling, always taking the side of man in his struggle to be, and opposing the forces within or without that oppose, or destroy, or degrade man. He was personal but indiscriminate, specific but nonaffectional.

Where does that leave us? It leaves us always dealing with specifics, in the aura of Jesus' love. To sharpen the point, we pose some propositions:

— Was President Truman right in ordering the Hiroshima and Nagasaki bombs to be dropped?

— Is it ever right to be involved in extramarital sexual intercourse?

— Should a person lie to protect job or family?

— Is moral compromise ever justifiable?

In these four queries, one specific (because to date, as far as we know, there has been only one of its kind), the others general, we have stated the main ethical curiosities of our day. Mass killing, sex, lying, and, lastly, the possibility of bending taboos to meet the occasion are the areas in which most people will raise questions and will fear that subjective relativism could lead to anarchy.

The answer to all four questions is, " Quite possibly." It depends on the circumstances, the people involved, and what the loving act really is. As for the use of the atomic bomb, probably the most debated decision in history, there are many factors, some of which can be known only to Mr. Truman himself, and even these may be obscure to him. But we can at least imagine and try to see some of the major factors he had to consider. Since no strategic decision in warfare can possibly be clean, that is, avoid terror or killing completely, we see that his was a choice between already vastly tragic alternatives. At this point all we can say is that *possibly* it was a loving decision. But at least we have said that, and have not come to the final exclusive judgment that a complete pacifist, or some legalist, might. Because there was wrong in either possibility, that is, human suffering and degradation, neither choice could be called " wrong," rather, more or less advisable. And there is the probability that Mr. Truman's choice was the more advisable, therefore the more loving, thing for him to do.

The matter of sexual involvement is as complicated as life itself, for there are myriads of different kinds of relationships. The point has to be raised, though, in the light of the Judeo-Christian taboos that have drawn such clearly definable lines of judgment. The tradition is simple in its structure: all sexual relations outside of marriage are bad; all those within the covenant of marriage are permissible. This could *only* be a vague and idealistic guideline; it is too simple and too unyielding in its confines. Sexual intercourse is the most intimate, the most powerful, and the most potential of all human relationships, and as such will, like human fingerprints, always be different in each case — *each* case. There is no umbrella morality to sex. Where it is the expression of love, always characterized by responsibility and justice, it will be a supreme exposure of humanity. As such, it is good. Where there is a debasing of the personal values, an exploitation of people to attain sensual pleasure or power or gain, it is unloving; this can happen frequently within marriage. Chapter 6 will have more to say on this subject.

The Christian, therefore, looks upon marriage as a respectable and possibly honorable institution, but the morality of its sexual aspects will have to depend upon the persons involved and what they are really trying to communicate to each other in the sexual act. For sexual intercourse, in a person-centered viewpoint, is basically an instrumentality of communication, in which two people who are responsibly committed to honoring each other seek to confirm and assure the validity of the commitment. And this can exist outside of marriage, with circumstantial difficulties. Karl Barth speaks with great pastoral wisdom when he says, " Coitus without cohabitation is demonic."

In the related problem of prostitution, the question to be asked still pertains to love. Why is the woman renting out her genital organs? Is there an element of service or loving sacrifice? Are there those who benefit from this? We know just enough about certain isolated instances to say, " Possibly." It's most likely rare and exceptional, and in most cases prostitution contributes more to depersonalization than to love. (*That* ought to lessen the panic of the legalists!) But the difference between saying that much and saying that prostitution is always wrong, always immoral, is as vast as outer space. The fact that Jesus refused to treat prostitutes as any less human than any other persons is supremely important to those who follow a positive ethic.

By now we see that the matters of lying and compromising also fall within the range of ethics in context. The chances are quite high that everyone who speaks or writes indulges in subtle

falsehoods daily. The hairsplitting work of differentiating between an exaggeration, an enthusiastic sales pitch, a deliberate
misrepresentation, or consistent untrustworthiness is no business
at all for ethics. The call is to say that which is loving; the facts
often are not the best or the most accurate representation of
the truth. When a fire breaks out backstage in a crowded theater, it may be factual for the manager to shout the information
to the audience; it may be far more loving to make a calm announcement that " due to a small problem " it seems best for
the people to leave the theater calmly. The law of the State of
California, as well as that of some other states, provides for the
expunging of misdemeanor arrests from a person's record, so
that he may answer employment application questions on previous arrests with a legal " No." Certainly the husband's adoring, " You are the most beautiful woman in the world " is a
loving and passable bit of prevarication. If these are justifiable,
then advanced degrees of the same thing, in the light of the
desperation and the intensity of human values involved, are too.

These examples are not laid out to defend lawbreaking. This
isn't a defensive chapter. Rather, we are describing to ourselves
the freedom of manward love. Law, habit, tradition, can all be
prisons within which the human spirit is forced to cringe for
security, or they can be footholds from which love marches
forth to ennoble its own. The leaders of the American Revolution lived in a society proscribed by law, based on a British
heritage in which the person had always been important. But
their experience was clouded by distortions and exploitations
of that very tradition. Did they strengthen, or destroy, their
grand British heritage by revolting against it? Did they ennoble,
or degrade, the suppositions of Western civilization by opening
fire at Concord bridge on their brothers? Objectively and legal-
istically, it was as brash and disobedient a violation of the civil
order as, say, the Russian to-do of 1917. But we look back over
the softening years of history and cover it with a golden glow
of heroism, saying that tyranny must ever be treated so. Ergo,
law is subject at all times to love — no matter how harsh its

methods, or how offensive its mien.

Did Jesus respect the law? By all means; he stood in great appreciation of it, and vowed that not one " jot or tittle " would pass from it before the objective of human salvation was under way. He lived within the law for the majority of his teaching life, and used the law when it upheld his love that upheld man. But there were times when his expression of redemptive love soared above the law like an eagle over an ox. Was this breaking the law? Technically, yes. Operationally, it was using the intent of the law which transcends law itself. " The sabbath was made for man, not man for the sabbath."

But we digress. Love on the manward offensive is the motive of morality. Love on the offensive assumes that every human contact, no matter how apparently trivial, is an arena of unlimited potential for augmenting man's dignity. Love on the offensive means that he who loves carries into every incident an aggressive insistence on making every person understand himself more realistically. Manward love looks upon every confrontation as a moral decision of high intensity. It elaborates the significance of the telephone call to a hymn of praise; it sees in the parental rebuke a microcosmic fragment of God's grace, as in the Communion cup. It peers into the parked car in lovers' lane to behold the experience of a new self-realization that could unveil a heretofore frightened and withdrawn personality. An *ad hominem* love covers the bustle of the marketplace with an ill-concealed admiration for the richness and wonder of the constant game of bargaining and caring. Love on the offensive looks into the haunted eyes of the old, the bitter, the tired, and sees a depth and a mystery to which it yearns to relate.

Thus, in the dramatic scenes of moral decision-making, love on the offensive, like Jesus, operates on its own terms in the direction of man. At the well in Samaria, Jesus had already incurred the disgust of his followers by relating to even the village whore, a decision made at first sight. But he insistently continued, pressing his case for the release of the woman from her own self-disdain, and finally accomplishing it by exposing her and openly admiring what he had exposed. The store clerk who caught a customer doing a little shoplifting not only turned her in to the police and testified against her in court, but visited her in jail and later intervened with her own employer to have a job available when probation was granted. It was loving of the clerk to insist on a proper facing of the crime and its consequences; it was also loving of her to maintain a humane concern for the person. It was loving of King David to wrest the kingdom from the psychopathic Saul; it was also loving of him to invite the relative Mephibosheth to sit at his table for life. It was manward love that sent Florence Nightingale to the Crimea, Albert Schweitzer into the Congo, and Eugene V. Debs into politics. It was loving of some students at the University of California to put their lives and careers on the line to protest campus injustices; for others of their fellow students it was merely the exploitation of a dramatic opportunity to get a few " kicks." It was manward love that moved Philippine nationals to share their meager rations with American missionary prisoners in the Santo Tomas concentration camp near Manila.

It goes on and on. Our tremendous drives to adore and worship, to revere and respect, drive us far more than does physical hunger. We have looked all over the heavens for an object to adore and hold in honor. Jesus showed us the place to begin.

It was with our neighbor, all the time.

# 4

---

## THE COMPONENT PARTS
## OF AN ETHICAL DECISION

THERE ARE many myths about ethical decisions. The most constant one is that if one lives one's life along predetermined noble standards, morality enters the picture as though one were at bat in a baseball game. Some mysterious impersonal destiny or testing force keeps pitching predicaments at us, and we " defend " our morality by deciding in time whether to swing, bunt, take, or duck. Our " morality " is to be seen in our batting average, visible on the scoreboard of public reputation.

The mythness of this is seen in its passivity. Though we may not think so, ethical decisions are not so much thrown at us, or pop up in the course of life, but emerge from thousands of contributing factors. Not the least of these factors is the moral flavor we bring to the scene because of the kind of people we are. But the myth persists, and its inevitable logic would call for a set of prescribed rules which, if followed faithfully, imply being " right." Always swing on a low fast ball, step aside if it comes toward you, be sure to run if the catcher drops the ball on a third-strike call, and so on. Never steal, lie, adulterate, talk back, or use four-letter words. Always tell the truth (at least *you* will be safe), and be polite, reverent, and clean. The difficulty with this myth is that it turns out to be practical in only a small percentage of real-life situations. Most of the time when we think it is appropriate to make a decision, so many intermediate ones have already been made that moral ambivalence is the order of the day. And just when we need them, all our nice little propositions break down.

Another myth, somewhat related, is that right and wrong are as measurable as black and white. Regardless of long-range consequences, says this myth, it is our calling not to be troubled with the unpredictable but to make obviously proper decisions, and there is an eventual destiny that will accumulate the score and make everything turn out all right. After all, the emotional strain of trying to predict how it will turn out is too much for most of us, so we just have to do what we can. God, or Big Brother, or the State, or Fate, or Santa Claus is standing at a desk somewhere, keeping score of our obedience, and *that* is where we are really responsible.

The way people line up on both sides of the tangled problem of capital punishment is a demonstration of simplistic thinking. The issue has been thrown at us by history, law, and custom. Is it right or wrong? For most of the leadership on both sides, the reasons are clear-cut. It is right because the state can and should have the power of life or death, crime should be discouraged, and the wrong should be punished. For the others, it is wrong because the Bible says nobody has the right to kill. To move the whole center of gravity of the discussion over to an examination of each case would be to complicate it hopelessly, and no one seems to want to do it. Yet, in Christian terms, the matter is based not on right or wrong but on the appropriate way of dealing with persons. (In my limited pastoral experience, I was associated with a man who deliberately used the state as an instrument to commit suicide. He was, indeed, guilty of murder, but the element of alarm for me was that because the state had locked itself into an unyielding position, he could manipulate the law to bring about the very self-destruction he wanted. He had long since abandoned any idea of dealing responsibly with life; the state complied with his wishes, and an opportunity for society to experience a redemptive relationship was gone.)

That's the trouble with simplistic myths. They snuff out so many marvelous possibilities for us to explore the richness of loving through our confusions. And that, also, is the trouble with the question, What is the right thing to do? Notice that the subject of the sentence is *thing*. Ethical decisions are not made up of things, or principles, or laws, or guideposts. They are comprised of complex personalities with multicolored intentions and gradations of maturity, and all humanity trying to live through each episode with its sense of being attuned to life intact. Ethics is comprised of feeling, rebelling, hating, loving, caring, hiding, hurting, courageous people's jockeying positions with each other. It is on this level that the Christian faith puts together the dynamic moving parts of what most of us call an ethical decision.

Let us put together, then, as we can see them from Christian Scripture and experience, the things that produce morality and responsible decisions. Jesus seems to be far more interested in where we start than where we end up, and more interested in *why* we want to do something than in what actually happens. Therefore, taking the cue from his emphases, we can say simply that Christian decisions are composed of the Reason, the Strategy, and the Tactic.

## A. *The Reason*

Perhaps we should call it the Compelling Reality, because it is the heart of everything for the Christian and, as a matter of fact, has shades and echoes that rattle around in the psyches of those who would not consider themselves religious but who face mankind reverently.

It is the fact of Man. It is the tremendous pressure put upon every one of us to come to some kind of workable conclusion about this man. It is the necessity to make some kind of preliminary decision about man before any of us can have any kind of dealings with each other. We must know about our selves before any system of ethics can have any sense at all.

The reason this is important is obvious. If you are going to work with turkeys, you really have to have a rather elaborate rationalization worked out in your mind, justifying the concern for their welfare on the one hand and the methodical slaughtering of them for gain in the other. No one who deals with any living organism can help but develop a certain kind of relationship that either has to have its rationale or produce emotional stress. So the turkey grower explains to himself that the turkey, though a living thing and in some ways created in the image of man, is part of the creation that can be treated properly as food resource and, therefore, may be freely killed as the grower would never feel free to kill man. Sounds rather zany, yet sit around the fire with any old friend turkey growers you may have, and, if you press them just a little, you will get a confession that this very process is necessary.

Philosophy may be a remote-sounding word to many of us, yet the fact is that our every attitude has its subtle, unspoken supportive evidence lurking in our subconscious. We really do have to have a philosophy, or a rationale, or an explanation, behind everything, especially our interpersonal developments. If we think we don't, just scratch the surface of every attitude we have toward persons, animals, or things, and lo! There it is.

So, since ethical decisions always arise out of what takes place between people, or at least between a person and a problem, all such decisions have to start with our understanding of man. Even here we don't have to get too pedantic about it. We don't even have to feel that our vocabulary or our reasoning has to be very profound. The illiterate Mayan Indian that I met in the Mexican jungle had his rather completely worked out idea of man, coming to him from the traditions of an ancient and somewhat successful culture. Man, to him, was an order of jungle life whose value was in direct proportion to geography. Those close to him were to be loved and protected; those at an intermediate distance were to be exploited and suspected; and any beyond that range simply didn't exist. To him, I was a curiosity to whom he could relate congenially in passing, but I was not worth taking seriously, for there were far more important things to be bothered with. Besides, he knew that when he had lost interest in me, I would go away and simply not exist anymore for him. The ethical implications of this bring a whole host of taboos and retaliations for misbehavior, and emotional involvement, to the anxiety level concerning family and near friends, but such unconcern for the others as to make cruelty or even killing passing possibilities if annoyed. Just as javelinas are killed for meat, coyotes for protection, and ants for comfort, so are threatening humans. That's the order of things in which they fit.

Some hardened law enforcement officers see people as potential lawbreakers, all to be distrusted. Some tired schoolteachers see their pupils as a great horde of resistance, to contend with patiently, and if, mayhap, there be an encouraging puncture and some student respond with interest, it is a happy exception. The skid-row pawnshop keeper, crouching behind his wire cage, sees mankind as an endless procession of derelicts, clinging to the cliff of life by their dirty fingernails, to be neither exploited nor encouraged but just served on the basis of what junk they pawn for their booze, with a shrug of the shoulder and a " So goes it! " One nurse in a convalescent hospital for the elderly sees her patients as near-vegetables to be kept clean, fed, and shot. Another may see them as fascinating, challenging, admirable people whose illness and senility are problems to be faced on their behalf.

You can see that if you were to take the people mentioned above, and the several dozen you could add to the list, and mix up the different ideas of man, there would come an immediate shift in social behavior which would have ethical implications twelve feet deep all over the countryside. If the pawnbroker had the schoolteacher's eye, he might start relating as an educator instead of a businessman, or, if he had the nurse's viewpoint, he might try to act therapeutically. Those who came to his shop would find more than ready cash.

Enough with the ground-level examples. The same principle is to be found on other levels too. Nations have to style their political ideas around ideas of man. British colonialism, for instance, in some ways a child of the Christian missions, clearly felt that man was divided into three kinds, and each man could be treated in his own classification. There were the believers, the infidels, and the barbarians. Believers (Christian in one sense, loyal to European culture in another) were not only treated as equals but given ceremonial recognition at every turn in the road. Infidels (Muslims in the original sense; in the secular sense, the intermediate range who could be Westerners but weren't completely) were treated as equals on their home ground only. Whenever they came on British soil, however, they had to accept the consequences of being different (that is, inferior). The third range, the barbarians, were actually subhuman, always to be treated as hewers of wood and drawers of water, to be denied the institutions of advanced society (which "the dumb brutes wouldn't understand, anyway"), and always to be exploited "for their own good." Because of this strange trichotomy in a culture dominantly Christian, such an advanced people as the British could, on the one hand, be the agents of high idealism and nobility to the Western hemisphere and, on the other hand, promote so crassly the most degrading slavery. What is man? Well, say they, there are different kinds, you see . . .

Perhaps of all the systems in the modern mode, Marxism as interpreted by those nations which are consciously trying to be communistic has the most clearly stated doctrine of man. No divisions into classifications are possible here. In dialectical determinism, all men are equal, and this equality is one of the supreme facts about man. In reaction to the feudal injustices of the czars, no man is permitted to assume godlike status; therefore, the range of rights, or ultimate value of man, is limited to practically the lowest common denominator. Communism does not rule out entirely the idea of the soul or some kind of divine destiny or supremely endowed belongingness. If there is such a possibility, it can never apply to man in the singular — and suggestion of enduring value has to pertain to the state, or to man collectively. There *is* an element to revere and a reason for a mystique beyond the visible, but it is attributable to *society*, or to men rather than man.

With this basis, Communism can readily explain its freedom to destroy units of men without apprehension, insofar as they have become infections in the side of the near-holy state. The rationale here would be precisely the same one with which the Western world would encourage the amputation of an infected limb to save the life of a person. If man, indeed, is a contributory part of the divinity of the state, in his separated condition he must always be considered expendable with no remorse if the good of the state is at stake. This immediately directs that in all priority choices the integrity of the body politic comes first, and individuals, or the representative person, have no more claim to favored handling than does an agricultural commodity.

I am trying very hard here not to succumb to one-sided generalities. I have visited the Soviet Union and other Iron Curtain countries and have many warm memories of associations of honor there which deny everything said above. I have seen many ethical decisions made on a high plane of love and respect for human values that would shame most of us who live in what we oddly call the " free world." Yet there is an overall assumption, explicit in the ideology and obvious in the conduct of government, in which the position occupied by humanity in the specific is such as to permit degradations beyond belief for the confirmation of the state.

There are other systems of anthropology held by movements or groups in the world today. It would be easy to describe the understanding of man among the Black Muslims, the Ku Klux Klan (both children of the British colonial system), the labor-management polarity, nurses in a leprosy hospital, foremen of highway crews. The jarring self-immolation of the Buddhist leaders in Vietnam who seemingly destroy themselves for the good of other men may sound almost Christian in at least the heroic intent. However, the place and value of life in the Oriental contemplative system puts almost derogatory despair on the possibility of socially redemptive relationships. Buddhism has no image of an ideal, or even a tolerable, society. It throws its whole emphasis upon personal righteousness, in the form of enlightenment, and lets the structures of society fall into the decay they deserve. In an almost complete reverse from the communist system, Buddhist ideology exalts the unrelated individual and decries a society's even trying to have what must be doomed as vain values. In true doctrine, however, it is quite possible for a Buddhist to burn himself to death as a measure of gaining pure enlightened nonexistence for himself. It is not so much in compassion for an injured society as in protest against a system which threatens his individual right to seek fullness that he makes of himself a human torch. This can lead to an understandable, but to Western minds a somewhat quizzical, set of ethical developments.

All these reviews are preludes to a necessary examination of what is traditionally called the Christian doctrine of man, not that we all really hold to it or that anyone has ever really grasped it. It is the reason for the forceful thrust of Christianity into all parts of the world, and even though the missionary movement has been confused in some places, and impure everywhere, it has still addressed itself to all men with an intrahuman voice of respect that just has to have some kind of strong explanation. And it does have certain fundamental and rather profound influences on everything we have considered under the heading of morals.

The Judeo-Christian tradition propounds a concept of man and of the place of all humanity in time and space which is not only somewhat unique among the thought forms of this world but universal in its implications. We simply *must* acknowledge in passing that we here deal with a contribution to the collective experience of history, injected from a socially insignificant pocket of the near-Orient, which is truly amazing. It insists that there is something true about ourselves and about all men that we would never have concocted by ourselves. It exceeds our wildest fantasies and confirms our most dismal suspicions.

This is what we call the Compelling Reality; it is the real scoop about man that is given to us in the Bible. It may, indeed, be the most workable bit of news we'll ever get from anywhere, and will affect not only our behavior but every attitude of hope, purpose, judgment. This picture, given in such majestically simple language in the Bible, has three legs, like the maiden's milking stool. They are known as Creation, Alienation, and Redemption, or, to put it in plain terms: we men have a purpose greater than the universe; we can't see or accept that purpose, but God can, and gently works to help us clarify our vision.

The first of the three is the belief that man, that mysterious, wide-eyed figure who resembles the animal kingdom so much and yet is a stranger to the other animals, much more strongly resembles that creative force which started the whole shebang. Of all the scenery of the universe, man stands on the earth, differing from his surroundings in a way that suggests a peculiar possibility beyond the stars. The image of God, the Bible calls it. Every man and all men begin their lives as heirs of a quality that includes a destiny; the difference between a man and his dog is not just that of form or language but that of the whole vast chasm of Person. We do not know what God is like, but we are given a feeble reflection of something quite undefinable about him in the persons around us. And even when we have assembled all that we know about everybody and try to piece together a mosaic that reveals God to us, we still don't know much at all; yet, we know something about man that has the ring of the divine and we can't let go.

This knowledge is not based on a hunch, or on a devoted and beautiful fantasy. This insight has come to us filtered through just about the most dependable process one could imagine, in which generations of people, frightened by the possibility of God and sensitive to his holiness, watched themselves and recorded their reactions. As their spirits tremblingly responded to the invitations articulated by their leaders to " draw nigh and know," they were almost overwhelmed with an involuntary reverence for the human. Conversely, when they withdrew to ways less threatening to their own self-labeling, they found they could be more arbitrary and cavalier about their brothers. And even though the majority consistently sought the latter path, there remained a significant, tantalized small group in each century who were awed by the sheer majesty and couldn't help seeing the glints of splendor in every man they met, friend or foe.

God made man and endowed his child with something of himself that makes those who adore God simply have to have reverence for men — *all men*. Aye, there's the rub. The bigger the idea of God grows, the wider the span of his loving creation and the more universal the inclusion. Whatever he put into you, me, my family, our inner circle, he put into all men: the Russians, the white southerners, the mentally retarded child next door, the crabby old lady in the county home. It was his idea, not ours. That's the way he did it.

Wherever there is a painting by Rembrandt, or a stained-glass window by Connick, or a building designed by Frank Lloyd Wright, or a car by Rolls-Royce, there is respect in the audience. It's not based on the value alone of the individual exhibit, which may or may not be something extraordinary. It's just that the touch of the master's hand has put something there that is the " real thing," and it will always be so. Even if we don't for the minute care for it aesthetically, we still have to admit that since it bears a resemblance to a concept in the maker's mind, it has an indescribable standing among men everywhere. To the Jew or Christian, every man is a product of unspeakable holiness, purposefully and personally put together for a reason that will outlive the light-years of space, and therefore is to be acknowledged as respectable as God is acknowledged as adorable.

Let's face it. The major reality for us all is creation. We *are*. Not only that, the characteristics of our existence continue to tickle the wonderments at the back of our minds. Prowling recently around the Southwest, browsing through the archaeological footprints of the pre-Columbian Indians, I was again confronted with the evidence. A people so different, so remote, living in cliffs in primitive self-protection societies, worshiping their nature gods, bound by fearful superstitions: they're not like me at all. Yet, compared to the other orders of life, to the grazing antelope, to the scampering lizard, to the growing maize, we are brothers! We are made in the same pattern, with the same creative yearnings, the same needs. They developed language to communicate, families to propagate, taboos to legislate, even apartment buildings and communal structures to domesticate. Obviously they, and we, are both reflections of *something*. And there is just enough of a suggestion of vitality in each of these clouded reflections to tell us that our originator is Life above all the dimensions of death. Because *that* is so ennobling to all that is in our sphere, each piece of humanity is supremely important to us. "How can you say you love God whom you have not seen, when you cannot love your brother whom you have seen?"

The second leg of the stool is what the modern cynic would call "realism." It doesn't take the doubting world to throw a handful of mud on the somewhat rosy and pink-cloud idealism of the "image" idea. The Bible has already done it; as a matter of fact, it moved rather rapidly in its opening passages to make the point painfully clear. The emphasis is that if man really is made to look somehow like God, he certainly doesn't let it stand in the way of his galloping gladly into a resemblance of the animals around him. The story of separation, the Garden of Eden allegory, puts the whole predicament as clearly as any scorner could: since man has the freedom of personhood and his choices are respected by all creation, he early developed the habit of choosing to be impure and unholy. And he does this without too much remorse.

As a matter of fact, the Bible makes sure this theme is never forgotten, that humanity seems to be as capable of the bestial and demonic as creation itself. The extents to which we seem to go, both collectively and on our own, to disprove any relationship at all to the eternal or to the loving are factually much worse than our most depressed pessimists want to describe. We have insulated the memories of Buchenwald and Hiroshima and the Marne and the Crimea and Shenandoah and Bull Run in a rosy romanticism of " noble " warfare, but we can never deny that these occurred in " advanced " civilization. We are at a loss to explain the moral failures of good men, of Teapot Dome and vicuna coats, of cheating at West Point and dishonesty by public servants. We shrug our shoulders and mumble something about being " only human," but the point is that we are too hurt by our own shallow idealism to realize that it's all been said already. The loveliness of the first point, man's nature and his resemblance and his destiny and his potentiality, is blurred and distorted by the obvious truth of the second — blurred and distorted, that is, not denied, or negated, or canceled.

The same Bible that told us of the first told us of the second with equal candor and honesty. They are both true and, as a matter of fact, both a matter of common experience if we but look for them. The two stand as a description, though not an exhausting confusion, and always on the brink of a despair too yearn for the best for all and, in the same moment, hurt and betray and destroy beyond any credulity. *It's true.*

One of the dominant aftereffects of World War II, with its horrible revelations to man of what man can do to his brothers, was a widespread disillusionment. So many came home from the twisted ruins and piles of stinking corpses with a sardonic view of creation that despair colored the air everywhere. The bearded nonconformist in Greenwich Village, searching for his " identity," the doctor in Texas who limits his emotional life to drugs and stitches, the rigid, overserious young man in Portland who is afraid of people, the brassy politician who maneuvers people with the glad hand and wide smile for his own glory, are all frightened, fragile little spirits who have been hurt by having their "druthers" about the goodness of man brutally overruled. And most of them are discounting religion as too naïve and unrealistic to meet the hard truths about this stinking old world. Presumably, God would be terribly embarrassed if he really knew what his children were like when his back was turned.

Yet it is the Bible, and the first few chapters at that, which straightforwardly tells us that we live in constant contradiction, exhausting confusion, and always on the brink of a despair too deep to heal. It is the Bible that watches the wobbly line of men going through their little exercises of faith and corruption, of love and cruelty, and that seems to describe what's going on without blind optimism or bitter cynicism. And it is the Bible, in the face of all this, that goes on to a third factor which man in all his sophisticated realism can't possibly conjure for himself. If it weren't for this, the very sensitivity to values and goodness and beauty to which we all respond with hope would have turned to ashes long ago, and we would have destroyed ourselves in bitterness. Some men do, but, strangely, most of us want to carry on.

This is that all-important part of understanding man to which our religious tradition gives so much tender attention. Here we are given an invitation to hope, not just for endurance or survival, but for fulfillment of that splendor which is in our creation. For as the years go by, mankind is led to believe that though he may give up hope for himself, God leans toward him with a healing intention. What this means, how it is going to work out in history (if it ever does), and how it works out in our individual lives (if ever), we do not know. We are simply invited to see the actual earthly experience of those who saw Jesus the Christ in person and who beheld there a reason to keep looking for God to act that way everywhere. We talk about "salvation" and "righteousness" and the "Holy City" and the "eternal Kingdom" and the "forgiveness of sins," not really knowing much at all about what they mean. But we do talk about them, and hope for them, because we feel we have been invited to do so by someone who knows a great deal more about them (and about us) than we do.

When one reviews the way in which God has " leveled " with us in the Bible about ourselves, one sees that we have been told about everything we can handle. The three truths together comprise the real dope. The first gives us a basic price tag so high that we are dazzled and excited, so close to answering that restless searching within us for a sense of cosmic recognition that it leaves us breathless; the second holds up a mirror of devastating accuracy before us which is so merciless in its hard factuality that we are nearly destroyed. It says what we may have suspected and become a little sober about, but it almost says too much. So it is the third truth that restores us with a wistful, only too fleeting call to hope and work for being rescued from ourselves.

The result of this triptych makes us look out upon the face of the anonymous crowd with terribly mixed emotions. We know that each person there stands within a family circle of great belongingness, that very same family to which we belong with gratitude. Without knowing we belonged, how could we possibly stand the loneliness? And that very same loneliness could be our brother's destroyer just as it could be ours. We are bound together, whether we want to be or not. If we find ourselves not wanting to be, there is a sense of alienation that disturbs us unaccountably. In the same glance we know that these, our brothers, can't be trusted. They are just as estranged from us as we are from them, and in their struggle to stay in their protected niches, they could hurt us even as they could love us. We also know that we too are broken fragments, and could betray and destroy even though we may be telling ourselves we don't want to. This is our conflict, and all men's: we share the same glory and the same desire to shrink from that glory. We rejoice that they and we are heirs of the best, but then we have to be practical and use good common sense and protect ourselves. Men may be of a divine creation in the abstract, but in the specific they can hurt like hell. So don't get too close!

It is that third item, that all-important third assurance, which is so very necessary in this symbolic glance we are taking at humanity, which becomes the peculiarly driving, compelling, inevitable, and inescapable dynamic to all that we do about life. If God hasn't given up hope on them, and on us, then we don't have the right or even the alternative to give up either. If he can still see the unmarred perfection somewhere in that mass which he put there in the first place, if he can see something for which to pay some kind of cosmic price that compares to the earthly pain of the cross, then, when we look out at the despicable, we too can see the lovable. It's not our show and it's not our noble ideal; it's the irrefutable truth of it all. If it's at all possibly true about us, it *must* be true about all humanity. The one thing we have to hang on to is that it's something we all have in common; therefore, we, you and I specifically, cannot by our own action disqualify ourselves from the intention that all men be saved.

Run this through your mind several times, and it may serve to bleach out the fragile piosity of love as an ideal. If there is any authenticity at all to this viewpoint, then to be a loving person has no great virtue in it; it's just unavoidable. Not to want to be loving is another way of running and hiding from everything for which we live. It's like being raised in an English-speaking household in an English-speaking country and deciding that it constitutes too much of an invasion of your personal privacy to bother to learn the tongue. It brings the desired insulation, of course, but it's somewhat unrealistic.

We have here talked as though a doctrine of man was a process of logic based upon information dropped from heaven which we must swallow to be " in." Using such words as " doctrine " or " concept " as we have is an intellectual and semantic trap. The course we have used really applies more to what goes on at a much deeper level than conscious logic. More than concepts, the insight about man really is the most effective at the " hunch " or motivational level, that attitudinal color which tinges the way all of life is interpreted. What psychologists and sociologists like to call a " scale of values " amounts to what the man in the street will call " gut-level " feelings.

How men come to this kind of insight yet remains somewhat of a procedural mystery. We cannot deny, however, that the presence in history of a continuing, worshiping community protrudes the farthest into a visible demonstration of it. We seem to arrive at our operational opinions of man through the context of our formative years, or through an experience of exposure such as worship. Those who have been in a loving community, or exposed to the act of spontaneous adoration that constitutes the heart of worship, find their kinship.

Systematic theology at best is the *describing* of what the church feels to be true. The ways by which it has come to this feeling far transcend the printed words of Holy Scripture or the cold facts of church history. These feelings have accumulated in what some call the " racial subconscious " and have become the abiding assumptions of Christian living.

All this is said to point out that what is told in these pages cannot be classed as a driving argument. We have simply looked at the phenomenon of Christian love and tried to point to the place, the Compelling Reality, from which it came.

So far, so good. Now what? We have a picture or, at least, some general suggestions of a picture that says some rather fantastic things about man — whoops! — about me. Now comes the step of becoming involved. The question presents itself: Now that you have an anthropology, what are you going to do about it?

No escaping it, at this point we arrive at a crisis. Shall we or shall we not admit to ourselves that everything which happens to us from here on out will depend on our reaction to this truth?

Remember King Canute, who refused to acknowledge that the sea would not obey his sovereign authority? He got wet. Remember General Custer, who couldn't accept the fact that a few untrained Indians could . . . You know how *that* came out! We could fill several pages with pathetic examples of those of us who faced a crisis of importance by denying it was there. This crisis is the one of seeing ourselves, and all men, as participants in a community and a destiny, or of discounting the whole thing. Unlike the result for Canute or Custer, our result will be simply that of living and not knowing ourselves or seeing the splendor in our brothers, but it's quite a loss.

We are pressed for a decision. Shall we respond with gratitude for that which is true about God, and about us, or shrug it all off? This is both a decision as to the stand one must take who believes thusly in man, and more than a decision. It is a direction of living. When a person says, " I accept Jesus Christ as Lord and Savior," he is committing himself to see the world and all men through the eyes of love, respect, and kinship.

Some concepts of man are not compelling. Once adopted, they permit the holder to operate as he always has, treating his fellows with the same disdain, or distance, or tolerance, or courtesy, or cruelty, as he would anyway. But that, in a sense, is exactly right. We respond to our brothers in the very dimensions of our opinion about them; if man is not important or useful, we can take him or leave him as the situation commands. But if man is that high reflection of the holiness of the universe, we must make a treaty with ourselves about the meaning of every relationship. Every confrontation, however casual, will have to be a crisis to the Christian because it will be a microcosmic rehearsal of what has happened to him at the altar. It does not matter *who* the man is.

So this calls for an ordering, a decision on direction. And *this* is where, in the putting together of the parts of an " ethical decision," the actual decision or volitional choice is made. The choice is not what to do but whether to love, not how a situation will work out but whether to honor all men everywhere because of their high importance to God. Whether men in their different individual units mean very much to you emotionally at the minute is not important. It's what they mean to you *substantively*. It doesn't matter whether you are particularly happy about the sunrise; it may be golden and inspiring and invigorating, or it may be dull and depressing. The fact is that it is bringing you a new day and you have to face it with some kind of living. You'd jolly well better have a direction of some kind to take in it, for a day is a crisis too.

After we have discovered what it is about humanity that one will accept as a working description, one's determination to face mankind and to participate in it in the light of one's belief is the beginning of all morality. It is on the sharp spine of this watershed that a theology has anything to do with ethics, and it is here, not in the making of field decisions, that there is any moral relevance at all. Here it is that the contrast is seen between commitment and convenience in a system of standards. The dominant whites of Rhodesia, South Africa, Alabama, and the segregated everywhere acknowledge by their *position* rather than by their *decision* that they feel no compelling commitment to a Christian doctrine of man when it interferes with a protected expediency. But in their midst, blood of their blood and flesh of their flesh, are those who have made the connection between a doctrine and a commitment, and who stand bravely for the proclamation to the world of human dignity in the specific. Alan Paton has his ilk — few, to be sure; a certain hardware merchant in Montgomery manages to keep his business going on an integrated basis but at a great price. His nonmartyrish comment: " They're human, aren't they? What else can I do? " Don't call him noble; he's simply realistic. A mortician in Southern California refuses to do business in the usual way; he is only too well aware of the emotional advantage the occasions of his contacts with clients give him. Instead of a padded, all-inclusive " fee," he itemizes for his customers the actual cost of casket, embalming, hearse rental, etc., and adds an unconcealed amount of his profit. It still totals considerably less. His comment: " I can only treat them as I want to be treated when I am too grief-stricken to be careful." It's neither heroic nor especially praiseworthy. He just lives with a commitment that arises from seeing man in proper perspective.

Briefly put, what we have talked about as the Compelling Reality is an honest description of us men, what we really are, what we are intended to be. The only way our systems can stand the shock of this frank information is to be involved in the divine characteristics of love. Now we move on to the human indications of love.

## B. The Strategy

Love can't be defined. But we have to describe it because we're talking about it. We know that it has something to do with an all-inclusive commitment to expose the integrity of all men, using the one closest at hand. We know that it is based on a creation which resembles what is Most Pure, and that it is our calling to relate to that resemblance in all men, first and foremost, above all other characteristics. But these aren't definitions. We can only really talk about love by studying its operational dimensions.

Love is seen to be authentic by the way it fixes on its targets. The lover is involved only because he loves, not because he figures to gain from the loving. Love is seen in the manner in which the targets are loved, and in what channels have to be taken to carry it off.

He who loves has a strategy that always has two points of reference: the person(s) immediately involved and the larger picture of mankind, or society, or " everybody's good," or whatever you want to call it. We'll call it the near frame and the larger picture, as though we were peering through the sights of a deer rifle, which has its own sticky ethical implications which we won't go into here.

It's that near frame, the " drawn bead," where love begins to be operational. The person being waited on in the dry goods store, the other driver on the freeway, the fellows in the car pool, the attendant at the service station: none of them has given special cause as to why they should be loved; none has really shown that much concern to think that being loved is an important part of your relationship. But then, of course, that's love, in an active ethic. It is there before anything else is going, and it sets the tone for anything that may develop. No one deserves to be loved; all people are the already-created targets of love merely because of the fact of creation. He who loves brings to every human contact a whole host of intentions to respect and reflect justice; he who does not love is already on the ethical defensive.

But it's that near target which gives all the trouble. Love is much easier as a general principle — it gets into all sorts of complications when it becomes specific. People are safe from a distance, since they come in assorted kinds of lovability. It's nice to say everybody has his rights; it's difficult to be impartial when some are friendly and others hostile. Will Rogers said, " I never met a man I didn't like," but he didn't cotton to everybody with the same warmth, as none of us does.

But therein lies the trap — to say that love is conditioned by the kinds of people to be loved. It isn't love that's conditioned, it's the expression of love. You may say a brusque hello to the janitor on the way to your office, give some snappy dictation to your secretary, and then have a relaxed and informal lunch with your colleague, being three different personalities in transit. But that doesn't need to imply that you love these three targets differently; it only means that there are appropriate ways of relating which differ. If you have a love ethic, all three of these people have the same priority of human importance to you, and any decisions you make will be motivated primarily by love in action.

For it is that target, that near frame, that specific example of what loving is all about and what it involves, which is your opportunity to live. First of all, he *is*. Being wasn't his fault or his idea; it was that same mysterious gift which came upon us all. Being came from that Somewhere in which the only effective reality is love, and which levies upon us no other alternative. To be is to love. Not to love is not to be. Those specific persons around us *are*. They exist. Not to love them is not to live. To love them is simply to make operational the fact of being. It's not a matter of choice, or of nobility, or of sentiment. It's just the only reality.

Love is not selective in its targets. If it *is* selective, it is not love but an empty defensive rehearsal of what life might be like if we could call all the shots. We can't, so love can't be discriminatory. The rude Puerto Rican who jostles our elbow on the subway and responds to our protests with an obscenity is a rather easy target to resent (an honest reaction), but resentment doesn't necessarily negate love. And if resentment is our only response to him, we have, ourselves, become somewhat less than being. Resentment will hurt us far more than it will hurt him. Should this disagreeable incident be carried further into violence, should he give a shove or take a swing at our collective chin, we may be moved, perhaps justifiably, to react in violence and clout him a solid throck on the proboscis. And that may be all there ever is to that relationship. But we still have the mandate to love, which will involve our own internal assessment of him, our acknowledgment of his valid existence, and a somewhat conscious concern for his eventual well-being. Whether or not it is followed up by some remedial action on our part — and we would just as well like to forget the whole mess — our active ethic of love will call for a loving reaction within us that will put us back in balance in relation to all men, of which he is a significant representative.

The distinguished author and teacher, John Bodo, has said that if the Good Samaritan can be praised for his acts of compassion and ministry to the injured traveling salesman, and if he were indeed a loving man, there is more to the story. Anyone who would stop and share his wine and his beast ought certainly to get a few petitions going to put more men on the Jericho Road Highway Patrol!

Perhaps the people who give us the greatest difficulty are the ones who are constantly in our scope of living, but on a minimal plane of personal interest: the milkman, the mailman, the business associates, the neighbors around the corner, the faces that only remotely have names but are seen frequently. Some of us have been drained by pouring large amounts of emotional juice into possible involvements that have led to rejection or to not being taken as seriously as we want. We have looked for recognition and affection in many directions, only to find that no one seems to want that kind of interest. And so we have withdrawn into our shells, like the cartoon of the nude man in the box, grumbling, " People are no damned good! "

Yet, substantively speaking, this is what life is all about. Within the fringe are those whom we love and who are gratified by sensing a strong reciprocal acceptance. " Home," said Robert Frost, " is the place where, when you have to go there, they have to take you in." And far beyond the fringe are the crowds with whom you have no immediate obligation to become involved. But it's the midrange, the casual acquaintances, the non-obliging but ever-present, which present the greatest challenge to ethical honesty.

It is quite right to say that there is a great difference between liking and loving. They are as different as an apple and an orange. They involve very diverse ranges of reasons. " Liking " does indeed depend upon attraction, likability, personality, appearance, usefulness, ideas held in common, ability to get along, etc. Loving derives *only* from the common belongingness to humanity. It is possible to love without liking. We do it all the time. But not liking cannot be an abandonment of the responsibility to love, and it quickly becomes a defensive position when it is confused with loving. None of us would find it easy to like the rough guy on the subway. But loving would include wearing his moccasins long enough to realize something of the inevitable hostility that minority groups cannot repress, of the frustration of those who live in a land of promise and see the daily breaking of that promise. We can go home rubbing our swollen jaw with indignant spirit aflame; yet, we can be filled with a sadness that tragic injustice is such an evident reality in this particular man's life.

We may not especially like the elderly lady who is so abra-

sively demanding of service in the restaurant that nearby customers are made uncomfortable, but in love we would be doing
our own spirits serious damage by writing her off. We may feel
sorry for the waitress who has to take the badgering and may
want to comfort her with an encouraging word. Our " liking "
her has made us resentful of the loudmouthed customer. But
we must not get thrown off our ethical aplomb by liking the
likable and disliking the disagreeable to the extent that our
love has also taken sides. Even just to assure ourselves by an
internal lecture that the little lady's rudeness may be really a
call for help, or an indication of desperate loneliness, or simply
residual bitterness that is giving her constant inner corrosion is,
at least, to exercise the surface symptoms of the love that puts
you squarely on her side in her fight to be. Not to see her as a
love target is the worst development of the day.

Liking is an emotion, a response to the people around us.
Loving is responding to existence itself. Honesty in assessing our
emotions is only sensible. Hostility, resentment, indignation,
even violence, are authentic expressions of emotional reactions
and ought not to be considered as negating love, or making it
impossible. Love is rooted in the whole person, whose different
parts are more than emotion, intellect, will, soul, and spirit.
Therefore no weakness in any part, or in all parts, can destroy
the reality of a loving person. Factors can only obscure its valid
expression. So anger, vengeance, fear, vacillation, even what is
publicly seen as immoral behavior, can be passing characteristics of the loving person, indeed, have to be because of predicaments coming from our created entrapment. Yet love can
find its way out and, in some cases, even use negative aspects
of personality to its own ends.

The stern disciplinarian in the military school, whose unbending allegiance to the rules is obsessive, may turn a deaf ear
to the lad whose feet are covered with blisters. He may order
him into the training march, yet still with a loving intent. Over
the tears and complaints of the boys, he may see the larger
good of giving them a dose of the system extant in the outer

world where no excuses are heard. The foreman on the construction job may use abusive language and Simon Legree tactics to make his crew get its work done, but he may be matching up to his own integrity, getting a high quality of work done, and relating to his men in masculine honesty. The lady bank cashier whose menstrual period always brings an emotional instability may be more loving in giving way to a shortness of temper with her co-workers than in repressing it to her own excessive fatigue. The aircraft engineer who is offended by his boss' bad breath may be more loving in telling him to brush his teeth or keep his distance than he would be in griping about it in the coffee lounge.

But when we have described the emotional setting of liking and loving, we have not yet said all that needs to be said about the fixation that love has on persons. The target of loving is specific samples of humanity, and loving is only to be found in living situations, not in principles or laws. It's like electricity, which is invisible and nonpresent until it is flowing through a turned-on bulb or appliance. There is no such thing as electricity in abstract; it can't even be said to be a reality. It only exists when it is operational, with specific local sets or machines responding to its power. Even the quiet, low-drain movement of an electric clock tells of a reality that just isn't when someone trips over the wire and unplugs it. There is no such thing as a loving person who isn't in the process of loving. It's a contradiction in terms. This is why Jesus insisted on coupling the admonition to love God — an abstract — with the direction to love the neighbor — a worldly specific.

A collective example is the racial problem in the United States. Far more people are proclaiming the necessity for racial fairness than are personally involved in bringing it about. " I think they're all right in their place. They have their rights. They should have housing and education and jobs, and I'll vote for it anytime." As for putting that noble generality into evidence, most people would think that the saying of it was enough. When, in the election of 1964, the people of California voted by a substantial majority to amend the constitution to permit "absolute discretion" in housing, they were saying in the privacy of the polling place that they were satisfied with the generality and wanted legal protection from letting it get any closer. Far more honest was the Georgia restaurant owner who not only resisted the "public accommodations" section of the Federal civil rights legislation but closed his eatery rather than serve Negroes. One cannot help but wish that the rest of the nation would converse as honestly about its feelings. No wonder the people of the State of Georgia elected the restaurateur, Lester Maddox, as their governor!

Erotic attraction and the confusion of genuine love with sexual feelings is an area of great importance. To tell a high school senior whose glamorous date offers no resistance to his advances that love begins in the here and now may give him the impression that he is getting a moral green light to proceed with some backseat joy. We have already pointed out the impossible hypocrisy of an absolute rule on sexual morality, and in the very saying of it we have opened the door to admitting that something very authentic may well take place in a backseat. Obvious as that may be, it is also obvious that the tendency to erotic satisfaction tends to be, in a majority of instances, a far cry from love. It is straining quite a bit to suggest that a teen-age boy has the emotional maturity to be objective and nondiscriminatory in his expression of love, especially with a delightful sample of perfumed fluff in his arms. Yet it is not unrealistic to suggest that the very same boy can have such a genuine and altruistic desire for the welfare of his feminine friend that his amorousness is only one, perhaps not the chief, method of communicating his interest. It does happen, you know. This is not to say that to proceed with sexual intercourse is always wrong in this instance, though it is probably inappropriate. It is to say that a fellow could be a real hero by making the girl feel more like a person than a thing, and this is far more possible in that context by restraint than by passion.

Some women who never rise above the rank of mistress in the

public eye make their whole supportive affections available to men who, in turn, can love their world more genuinely because of them. It may well be that because of the social sacrifices made and the extent of the risks involved, some people love more genuinely this way than in marriage. And, in turn, there are some understanding wives who acknowledge the place of a mistress in their husbands' lives as being authentic, and in love permit the arrangement.

A certain man was the victim of the birth defect, cerebral palsy. At the age of thirty-five he had learned to walk in a clumsy shuffle and to talk with a stammering, untidy cry. Asking favors from no one, he had managed to build up a business selling papers and magazines and had become a respected, though mostly just tolerated, member of the community. Another man, born the same year with the same defects, was still confined to his wheelchair and was an uncommunicative human vegetable. The difference between the two was to be found in their care as children. One mother refused to be overprotective, forcing her son to crawl outside as a little boy, watching him pull himself up by the picket fence, seeing him fall frequently and painfully, expecting him to make his own recovery, never consoling him, and only occasionally encouraging him. The other mother was indulgent and never demanding. In the early years the first mother was accused of cruelty and neglect, the second praised for her heroic devotion. But it was the first mother who was loving, for it cost her far more in emotional pain to go through the necessary regimen for her son's growth, and the results speak for themselves. One mother was thinking of her son, the other of herself. One mother was thinking of the future, the other of her own image of herself as an affectionate and sacrificing mother.

Love is specific and the near frame, the person, is the target, or else there is no target and no love. And that's the first half of our strategy.

The second half is the larger frame, the far gunsight. No matter how much we may sentimentalize about the nobility of loving the nearest person, the ethical value has not yet justified itself until we consider the context. Love is, indeed, specific. But love is a mysterious element of relationships, and all relationships have to fit into society or, if you want to call it so, the "larger good." Just as love can't properly exist unless it has a specific personal target, it has no validity if it goes on with no consideration at all of man in totality. Whether an action is "right" or "wrong" depends not only upon the motivation of love for the particular persons involved but also whether it supports the fabric of morality that holds society together in confidence and safety.

This is probably a control point, the place at which many will raise their eyebrows when ethics seems to be relative. "It's all well and good to do something extraordinary in the cause of love," say the proper commentators, "but if you get away with breaking a law or doing something we've always considered immoral, pretty soon everybody will be doing it, and society will get hurt." Quite so. Although love comes in specific units, it cannot be isolated in self-contained, socially inconsiderate bubbles. This is where law enters the picture.

A system of public standards cannot exist without law. Law is the codification of agreed-upon safety regulations by which society tells itself of its own security. No culture should try to live without law; none ever has. Law is born in human collective experience and, therefore, is more valuable as a starting point for personal behavior than individual judgment anytime. If fifteen people have fallen off a cliff to their deaths and the ruling powers make it illegal to go close to the edge, it's much better to obey the law than to become case number sixteen out of curiosity or the assertion of individual freedom. Everybody knows that killing is somewhat inadvisable, that it's a good practice for communities to frown on stealing, and that the best way to drive through a crowded city is to obey the traffic lights.

It is also true that law needs to be taken seriously by individuals as suggestive for personal living. The laws against dishonesty in the marketplace are meant to suggest that we become trustworthy and thus give and receive greater freedom, whether or not we're afraid of getting caught if we goof. Even if you can't love or have no desire to exalt human dignity and only want living space for your own little burrow in the universe, it's best if you obey the law. That's the best guarantee that others will too and leave you alone.

So an outgoing idea of ethics has no criticism to make about law, or any intention to do away with it or disregard it. Ethics starts with a healthy respect and appreciation for law. But law is not ethics, nor does it even produce the ethical life. It only safeguards a society in which loving people can act ethically. In those situations in which a loving act may require the breaking of a law to be truly ethical, it is not in disregard or denial but in fulfillment of the real purpose of the law. When Jesus said, " I came not to destroy the law but to fulfill the law," he wasn't dealing in the mystic completion of prophecy but was establishing the fact that true ethical living carries through in expression what law can only start.

The relation of law to love is to be seen in the firing of a torpedo from a submarine. (Please don't comment on the militaristic terminology; it's only a word picture.) The submarine, representing society, directs itself to the target, assuming the direction it expects behaviorally from its citizens. The firing tube is law that describes and defines the way in which it expects the missile to go; it provides the guiding discipline. But, to achieve the goal, the torpedo after it leaves the tube must set its own computing and guiding mechanisms into action, traveling in the general direction the parent vessel has indicated but making its own specific directions as it goes. Law provides all the basic general orders for the torpedo, but once free of the ship the missile itself is expected to make the specific decisions correctly. Even if it has to change direction to zero in on target, in so doing it will be fulfilling the intent, if not the guidance, of the submarine.

The real air space of human living (or water space, if you please) always comes between the firing tube and the target, or from a society that is directed by law but trusts that decision-making involves considerations other than legality. The main force of law is to make the actions of men socially safe. The gap between safety and appropriateness has to rely on judgment in specific affected by the advice of law in general. No code is really law that prescribes every situation and denies the individual his power to choose in love; this is trying to cover the whole project with an inadequate tube. A submarine that puts its nose against the target before firing will blow itself up.

A man is driving his pregnant wife to the hospital, and in true husbandly fashion he is close to panic lest the baby come too soon. The pressure of feeling makes him want to run every red light, drive beyond the speed limit, and disregard all other traffic. He has only one objective: to get his wife to the delivery room in time. Yet law says that it is not only *required* that he obey the regulations of the road but that it is more *appropriate* for him to do so because of the risks involved. Better to have a front-seat childbirth than a messy accident with criminal liability and possible loss of life. In this case, the loving thing for him to do in the confusion and stress of the moment, *as it usually is*, is to act within the law. Thinking of his family's welfare here is also providing for the welfare of others.

A high school girl discovers she has syphilis. The law requires that a report to the public health authorities and an investigation of her sex partners be made so that the disease can be stopped from infecting others. She has her parents and her reputation, even her future, to consider. Argument could be made in both directions about the loving thing to do, but in this case the law which came into existence to protect the larger number of people is the more appropriate and mature choice to make.

A certain poster used in the instruction of drivers of military vehicles has haunted me for years. It shows a truck with twelve soldiers in back rounding a corner and a child playing in the road ahead. The instructions to the driver are clear and hard: " If you have no passengers, ditch the truck and save the child; if you have troops aboard, you have no alternative but to destroy the child." Cold-blooded as it sounds, it makes sense when all things are considered. It *has* to, I keep telling myself.

The poignant scene depicted in John Steinbeck's *Grapes of Wrath* comes to mind. It shows the impoverished migrant considering whether to steal a loaf of bread for his starving child. The larger issues don't seem to be in his mind at all, but they are there, nevertheless. If he were to steal it, he would have to live in a society in which stealing is a fact, and he has helped to imperil the welfare of all. If he doesn't steal, an innocent life will suffer more. Here law calls to the scene the stake of society's quality, and love, always specific, brings its motives for all the pieces of humanity represented. There is no answer to this dilemma which can be called " right," except that to steal defiantly and with hostility against an insensitive society would be damaging, as would a hardened denial of the child's needs for fear of getting caught.

Perhaps you can now get the picture of the two gunsights. The little one, the bead that points to the specific, is the person, always the special love target, and always the incarnation of every generality about humanity. The other sight, the general range finder, is the collective integrity and safety of mankind. Morality that sees only one without the other is undirected, perhaps even wounds the innocent. It is expected that in most cases it won't be too difficult to align the two sights for, at least, an understanding of the shot. But it is those acutely distressing situations in which the nearer and distant sights just won't merge that become what we like to call difficult ethical decisions.

A loyal employee is approached by the supervisor that he admires, only to be asked to help out in a quiet embezzlement. His alternatives are to play ball or lose his job. This isn't really a predicament yet, because all the honest marbles are on one side and the bad ones on the other. Add to it, however, the circumstance of a desperately ill wife who is being cared for by the company medical plan and whose security would go out the window if he were fired. Now it becomes sticky trying to fit the love for the near and the security of the many together. Whatever decision is made, one cannot turn one's back on a sense of responsibility for society's dependence on an atmosphere of reliability. Choosing one of the two sights always involves a lament for the one that has to be ignored.

The Bible is a product of people who are not unaware that this can happen, and there are some references of help. It shows us that there is a difference between *society* and the *state*. That is, formal law and its enforcement are not necessarily synonymous with the good of all. There can be unjust laws and unjust social orders. No society is divine. No code is infallible. The man who obeys the law blindly could be in just as much danger of being morally wrong as the transgressor. Paul could say, when idealizing in Rom., ch. 13, that everybody should "be subject to the governing authorities" who, he says, "have been instituted by God." But his own actions don't bear out the admonition, as in the riot of Ephesus in Acts, ch. 19. There simply are times when a discriminating ethicist has to choose for the good of society against one of its own laws.

Here the progression of the twelfth to the fifteenth chapters of Romans adds a helpful and not unmodern pathway. Chapter 12 establishes the supremacy of love and the clear priority for all Christians of the near sight — the person. It can well be said that this is a warmly humanity-centered passage calling forth the trumpets that sound the golden tones of interpersonal richness: "Present your bodies as a living sacrifice, . . . that you may prove what is the will of God, what is good and acceptable and perfect. . . . Let love be genuine; . . . outdo one another in showing honor. . . . If your enemy is hungry, feed him; . . . overcome evil with good." This is where the sensitive and outgoing moralist starts, polishing up that near gunsight to look like a sparkling diamond, making the exaltation of the neighbor to be the greatest imitation of God.

But to stop there is to miss the point of a dialogue that Paul is having with himself for our benefit. The thirteenth chapter poses the other confusing and sometimes conflicting loyalty. It's rather arbitrarily put, and it makes rather clear that participation in political structures goes right along with the person. Certainly no one can say that historic Christianity is against the state, or for the repealing of all law! Even Blackstone himself (who once said that law should only reflect what society really wants) couldn't have been more adamant about the unbending importance of legal obedience. What is surprising here, if you are to treat ch. 13 by itself, is the intransigence of the apostle. A careful reading will show no loopholes of any kind to permit a conscientious Christian to go above the law.

This was the chief passage which was used by Hitler to subjugate the German church before World War II. The good people of Germany, who took their Bible seriously and who were convinced when the proof text could be produced, found they had no argument left when the Reichsfuehrer demanded their unwavering obeisance. As a governing authority, he was instituted by God. It says so in the Bible. So, at his direction, the life of the church (most of it, anyway) was conformed to the Nazi ideology, and the church became a footstool for the state. Many earnest people were greatly distressed about this and lived in untold agony of conscience, but they were gunned down by their own greatest weapon, the Word of God.

The problem was that they were studying the Bible vertically and ignoring its horizontal continuity. That is, they were stymied by a passage lifted out of the flow of thought, dismembered from the argument of which it was a vital part, and it proved to be a bomb to them. It is true, as refugees from the Hitlerian regime such as Barth and Tillich well knew, that Paul said exactly what is seen in this chapter, and that he rather forcefully overstated his case in order to make his reasoning watertight. The completing points for which these passages laid the foundation come in later chapters.

In ch. 14, the apostle tenderly begins to expose the incompatibility of chs. 12 and 13 by dipping into Jewish liturgical custom which had the force of law. Let's take, he says, a dietary proscription that is held to be a matter of important obedience for a good Jew. What is more important, the observance of the letter of the law or the possible development of a relation of honor and reconciliation between men? Who are you, he queries, to pass judgment? Now referring to the institution of the Sabbath, one of the most dearly held laws among Jews, Paul amazingly suggests that " everyone be fully convinced in his own mind."

Having warmed up on these sneaky revolutionary suggestions, the writer is able to point out that no law in the world can introduce the quality of life to be found where men are drawn to respect each other because of their respect for creation. The real climax of this passage of andante and allegro in crescendo comes at ch. 15:1-2: " We who are strong ought to bear with the failings of the weak, and not to please ourselves; let each of us please his neighbor for his good, to edify him." Certainly this is a high statement against defensive morality, and a proclamation of an ethic in motion toward man!

Not many years passed from the time of Paul to the time that Christians found themselves having to choose between making a symbolic acknowledgment of imperial divinity or maintaining an unpolluted witness to Christ. Probably there were Christians who took either way and lived to tell the tale; romantic history only remembers the martyrs. At any rate, it soon became evident that to quote chs. 12 and 13 side by side results in a ridiculous and meaningless dichotomy until chs. 14 and 15 are brought along.

The whole package, tied together without letting isolated verses fall out and start colonies of their own, goes this way:

> *Affirmation A:* Following Christ starts with a relationship of acceptance and mature love which is operational with me, vis-à-vis " all men." (Ch. 12.)
> *Affirmation B:* " All men " live in organized societies with laws and authorities. My loving them, then, will be en-

abled by "being subject" to those same laws and obeying them. (Ch. 13.)

*Affirmation C:* When A and B are in conflict with each other, both must be taken seriously, but the Christian is disposed to put the weight of his decision more toward A than B. (Ch. 14.)

*Affirmation D:* The Christian freedom from law, therefore, brings enormous responsibility to be directed by human values and a judgment system arising out of a sense of involvement with Christ. (Ch. 15.)

A child chasing a ball runs in front of a fast-moving car. To avoid the potential tragedy, the driver quickly breaks several laws. He drives over to the left-hand side, changes lanes without giving a signal, stops in the middle of the street. But of course there is no great ethical choice here. We have run down all four affirmations in a few seconds: reverence for the individual is of first importance; law is important to follow, but a situation arises where it is redemptive to break the law and save a life. This ought to be so obvious as to go without belaboring, but the projection of it into other dimensions blurs the certainty.

Take the two knotty problems of euthanasia and therapeutic abortion. At present the laws of the land, as well as custom and prevailing opinion, are very conservative on these matters. But so many cases appear to be borderline when it comes to actual justice (love) that those who work closely in medical or legal services find themselves emotionally torn. The law says that these are areas where man just does not have proper judgment over life or death; therefore, life, at any cost of human agony, is to be protected. But what's a doctor to do when he knows that the future holds no promise of anything but suffering beyond relief for months? How can he stay sensitive to the human elements involved when the law demands brutality? Will not more than one person be destroyed by a law that does not feel or cry out itself? Here the loving ethic calls for participation of excruciating vulnerability in love, and it is conceivable that the loving thing to do might in some cases involve break-ing the law. At this writing there is under way in San Fran-cisco a "civil disobedience" protest program by obstetricians, encouraged by an Episcopal bishop, no less, who are perform-ing illegal abortions in defiance of the law, both to uphold the human values involved and to bring pressure upon the law-makers to revise it. Inasmuch as they do it at great peril to their own careers and seem to have nothing to lose but their in-comes, it appears to be an exemplary demonstration of respon-sible freedom in love. And it is indeed a rehearsal of Affirma-tions A to D. Perhaps the most ethical thing to be said here is that every society ought to be able to provide room for this kind of demonstration, with ways and means of evaluating it on its merits and taking proper action. The real morality of the situation will not be found in its objective principles but in the intentions in each individual case.

Another widely discussed ethicolegal problem is that of wire-tapping. The Internal Revenue Service, it seems, has been sys-tematically invading the privacy of quite a few well-heeled citizens to make sure that they are accurate in their income tax reports. IRS says that it is quite justified in doing so, for dis-honesty seems to be rather widespread, the government is losing money that it rightly deserves, and besides, it only encourages further cheating to let so many get away with it. True, they have gone somewhat beyond what the law and good taste per-mit, but under the circumstances the welfare of the public makes the whole thing quite necessary. Opponents cry that freedom of speech and guarantees from self-incrimination are being violated and that constitutional rights are imperiled. A conservative pro-personal argument could aver that such a pro-gram is good for the individual in that it will encourage him to be as honest in private as he pretends to be in public. Whether or not the agency has any right at all to carry on such investi-gations, the question becomes very complicated when a certain agent is required by his superiors to be involved in the snoop-ing against his own judgment. For instance, it was reported that in some cases agents had to observe exceedingly private scenes, such as undressing and love-making, to gain needed information. How, in heaven's name, can you do your job " to the glory of God "? The honest thing to say is that some people do. Remember we have already said that there is no such thing as the luxury of a morally defensible position.

In proposing as a strategy the two-point " fix " for a moral position, the near and larger sights, we have used a neat figure which doesn't always fit that neatly. The list of affirmations from Romans is too pat to be easy and only amounts to back-seat advice. The truth of the matter is that the Christian life is an involvement in relationships that call for a living adaptability, a willingness to be used up for the honoring of all men, and the consequent pain of conflicting priorities. The poignant scenes of Dietrich Bonhoeffer's agonies while he was deciding his own fitness to help conspire to assassinate Hitler, in reality, depict the contemporary Christian in a thousand such scenes. Truly, Elizabeth Berryhill, author of the play *Cup of Trembling*, puts us all prone alongside Bonhoeffer in his garden; we well know what it is to be identified with man trying to choose the right from unclear alternatives. This, then, is a strategy: to see the individual and to see society and, in love, to bring that reflection of God's purity as we possibly can. But it still calls for a frank discussion of a tactic.

## C. The Tactic

Now we get to the subject that most people wish we would start with: what to do in any given situation. One would think that we have already established that this is not the place for absolutes. What? Can we depend on nothing anymore? Isn't right always right, and wrong to be avoided?

If ever there was a place for utter noncompromise, it pertains to the Compelling Reality and the strategy, but not here. For every arena of loving expression is different in terms of how the expression happens, but not in terms of what love means.

The context, or situation, or crisis, or whatever, always comprises at least two parts: the active and the passive. The active is that which the person brings to the time of "decision" in the way of moral force, or the already-made host of decisions about God, man, sin, and forgiveness. In a sense, these are the majority forces and also suggest that the "decision" has for the most part been made. An accomplished magician, teaching a class of beginners the arts of prestidigitation, revealed one of the important principles of that profession: "When the performer says, 'Now comes the trick!' you may be sure that the trick has already been done!" The explanation of that statement is simple. During the setting up of a switch, or the changing of cards in a deck, or the producing of a rabbit from somewhere, the magician carries on a line of patter that distracts attention from his hands or equipment. Then, when there is no legerdemain left to hide, he calls attention to his innocent hands and poof! Amazing!

When the back is against the wall, or the forces have come to dramatic collision, or the difficult choice seems ready to be made, in most situations the decision has already been made. The accumulation of convictions about the order of life brings a pressure of direction that supplies a moral momentum which produces the result. This is what we pointed out earlier about the life of Jesus; he carried his own morality into every situation and was never forced to make a decision defensively. It was the order of his life to direct considerable loving force manward which was never caught off balance. So it was that when the context provided no other way for him to manifest his active love but to go to the cross, he went, knowing full well why.

The passive element is the sum total of circumstances that come from other directions and are thrust upon the decider "beyond our control," another person's deliberate intervention, or beyond that whole complicated mess of society's anonymous problems. These words are being written on the 190th anniversary of the Declaration of Independence, a document of encouraging moral action in the face of oppression from overseas. None of the signers had much to do with the making of royal British policy, yet they had suffered for some time under the nameless injustices of the Crown. When these outward problems had become unendurable, the signers acted in concert on behalf of thousands to move decisively toward a freer and more just society, pledging to their commitment and its cost "our lives, our fortunes, and our sacred honor." In this case, the context included not only the dealings of history and a tyrannical absentee monarch but a community of sensitivity with a commitment above the immediate. The result cannot be categorized as "caused by" either the disordered gastric juices of George III or the nobility of the revolutionary fathers; it was rather the inevitable result of the active and the passive at the crossroads.

A common fault in all of us is to start our thinking about an "ethical decision" at the third component, the actual situation, and work backward to a relevant morality. This will always put us at the mercy of the forces of accident or of the strong and possibly demonic intent of others. This is why we tend to retreat into dependable hard-and-fast rules, because we are not prepared to deal with the context redemptively or do not have the sense of freedom to work it out on its own merits. We are driven to the defensive: lying is always wrong. Extramarital sexual intercourse is immoral. Violence is to be avoided. A policeman is always right. Even our pious utterances about God's will, or "we will rely completely on prayer to pull us through," have their elements of moral cowardice. When the context of a particular ethical choice is upon us there can be, and in Christian trust ought to be, a rolling impetus of morality that doesn't need places of retreat, but can carve from the raw material of what's going on, there and then, a form of expression that puts us on the side of man.

A minister has counseled with a parishioner who is a victim of epilepsy, though able with drugs to keep it under control. Although the man has not explicitly asked the pastor to keep the information confidential, both know that if his employer were to know, his job would be at an end. A few evenings later the minister is visiting in the home of the employer who is also a member of the same church. The boss makes no bones about it and makes no pretense at ethics. He asks the minister, " Does Jack have epilepsy? I heard a rumor and I have to know." The cleric is wise enough to know that if he hides behind his professional privilege, mumbling something about not being able to divulge that kind of confidence, it would really give the whole thing away. The questioner knows full well that the preacher has been told the truth, whatever it is, and stands ready to believe whatever the preacher says. If the minister tells the truth, a job will be unnecessarily forfeited, bringing considerable and unjust hardship. But he is not caught off guard. He entered the house knowing that a man's future depended on his being careful and loving with a high trust. Without hesitation he says, " No." And the matter is ended. It may be readily acknowledged that he had better alternatives, such as parrying the question with another question, but at that particular minute the moral thrust of his purposes was represented by what he said.

A " sweet young thing" chooses to go to a college whose reputation for student nonconformity is widespread. Though raised in a conservative household, the girl decides that her motives to gain an education include an objectivity about all the people with whom she is to associate. Soon after the beginning of her second semester, her roommate decides to live secretly off-campus with a boyfriend as a part of " making the scene," and asks her to cover up to make the project possible. A predetermined set of absolute principles would have brought the unthinking answer, no. On the other hand, an apathetic disregard for her friend could have brought a casual O.K. But this girl had already prepared herself for this very kind of situation and agreed to go along with the living arrangement only if the roommate would promise to confide in her clergyman and review with him the dynamics of the relationship. A year later, when she was herself involved in an erotic attraction with an assistant professor who invited her to live with him, she required of herself the same conditions and brought into the problem the elements of a constructive resolution.

It would be most misleading to give the impression that pre-thinking can guarantee the uncluttered morality of any decision. Nor should it be hinted that good intentions are all that matter and that what actually happens is ethically anticlimactic. True morality isn't at all interested in "justifying" any action by "meaning well" but, rather, in the best of preparations for the best to happen in authentic and loving relationships. The flow of thought here has been in the cause of setting the scene. It means making the major part of the decision before the context provokes the crisis of having to start from the beginning for a reason to love. Recently there have been two major shipboard fires on pleasure ships in the Caribbean. According to the newspaper accounts, the captain allegedly led the crew in a mad scramble for the lifeboats, leaving many passengers behind to perish. The second fire saw few fatalities because, said the reports, the skipper had made it quite clear to all what the procedure would be in case of an emergency, and how important the safety of every life aboard was to everyone else. So when the crisis came there was no need to stop and consider values and priorities, nor any need for self-centered panic. In both cases, decisions were made in quick order, and in both cases the prearranged order of survival was followed, the first being agreed upon implicitly.

No situation can be predicted. Nobody knows what ethical impasses are going to bedevil his path the next twelvemonth, and he only distracts himself seriously by trying to predict and prepare. But he can resolve to carry into each predicament an active element that points him in a certain direction, so that he is not completely helpless when the heat is on. He can also accept the reality that every action is going to have its high element of risk, sometimes acutely so, and he can come to a point of clarity in his thinking where he is at least willing to live with the risk without panic. This is the first part of the tactic.

It is the next, the actual moving into expression, the doing of the act, the making of the decision, that is the specimen on the slide in our ethical microscope. What is it?

Because this depends on judgment, skill, alacrity, alertness, experience, and a hundred other elements, what happens will *all depend*. In all such times it is the most advisable for one's thinking to begin with what we could call the traditionally moral. If the decision is one with varying degrees of dishonesty, the appropriate direction to swing is toward the least dishonest. If sexual behavior is in question, it is safer to stick to the lines of what is publicly considered proper. There *may be* just cause for the decision to be made in another direction — that may be the sum of all the contributing forces producing a loving conclusion — but *tactically* one begins to formulate the action on the accumulated wisdom of society. When it does become more proper to veer outside of custom, or propriety, or even law (and this writing is a witness to the necessary freedom to do just that), one has to be compelled to do so in love.

An attractive young divorcée with small children had conducted a most " proper " single life in her search for a new husband and companion. In fact, her behavior had been so good it proved to be quite lonely; she finally loosened up and found herself becoming too involved with a married man. One night, as she saw him playing with her children, she realized that she was very deeply in love with him and wanted to destroy his marriage so he could come to her. Frightened and dismayed by her insight, she resolved that she must put an end to the friendship and chose what seemed to her to be the only way to do it decisively. She threw herself at him " like a common tramp " (to use her words), dragged him off to bed and seduced him. In disgust, he returned to his family and never communicated with her again. Her tactic was one of desperation, serious risk, and questionable wisdom, but it was one of protection for herself and her children and, by good fortune, successful in its goal. She remained in an emotionally bruised and brooding state for some time after, but is thankful that the dangerous relationship is closed and "all hands aboard are safe."

If judgment were our place, which it is not, our counsel would be along the lines of the appropriateness of the tactic, never upon the morality of the purpose. We might suggest to her that in another time and another situation there may be less risky alternatives, but we have no justification for weighing the morality of her act because the intensely demanding life involvement, loving considerations with which she was dealing at the time were not ours, and we can never see what she saw. We can, however, extend to her and to all of our kind who find themselves in distress our commendation to act in love.

Some of us are more skillful in fielding the problems that life throws at us. That's all there is to it. Some are gifted with quick minds and tongues, and others aren't. Some of us can maintain our ethical demeanor with admirable cleverness; others aren't at all creative and tend to lose what objectivity and creativity they have in the pinch. This doesn't have anything to do with morality. A person can be a totally committed, divinely loving soul who is tactically clumsy. And some of the most adept have their times at making serious errors. Even Willie Mays occasionally bobbles a ball, and the best batting averages in the world level out at clouting the horsehide rightly only every third time at bat. It appears to be quite unsafe to draw conclusions about a person's "morality" or "goodness" or "rightness" on how he came through one, or even a few, critical times. This is probably the point of the Gospel story's making such a dramatic production of Peter's denials. They were tactical thoughtless goofs, showing only that this apostle, later to be considered chief of them all, couldn't think on his feet very well.

If some historian wanted to capitalize on this truth, he could fill several volumes with records of the misjudgments of great men and still have enough examples left over to paper the walls of his study. It would have a certain value, at least that of making us all feel a little better about our own unnecessary re-morse. Those of us who get some enjoyment from writing do appreciate the confession of Harry Emerson Fosdick that there was one book he wrote (during World War I, justifying Amer-ica's moral right to retaliate for German atrocities) that he wishes was never published. At least the miscalculations of most of us aren't embossed in print and preserved for nosy re-searchers!

Reassuring as all this is, we still have to admit the urgency that some of our tactics turn out to be responsible, enduring, and really being the channels of an ennobling love. This again is an argument for following the more traditional lines of moral-ity; the tactics didn't come from theory and pious imaginations but from ages of heart-hurting experience. As Lowell said, "New occasions teach new duties," and we would be of all men most stupid to let tradition take the place of God when the call was on us to be loving. So could Luther say, *peccate fortiter*, " sin bravely," and know jolly well what he was talking about.

When we say, as we have said, that one must be committed to a love for any man who, in the heat of battle, insists on standing for all men, and that one must then tend to do that which is traditionally approved, we haven't said everything yet. Under the heading of tactics we not only have to consider the goal — honoring all men — and the act — doing that which in this time and place gives honor to all men — but also the price and how far we are willing to go. In the example of the young divorcée, the price was living with the memory of what she had done and how she would be able to stand the rejection she had so unwillingly sought. A tactic of " doing what seems right in love and letting the chips fall where they may " is impulsive, infantile, and irresponsible. And any time we choose a tactic that is a nonconformity with law or custom, we can be as-sured that the price is going to be considerably higher.

This is not to suggest that the price of loving may be too high. It will always be high, and the more responsibly we are able to be involved in love the more it's going to cost. The question is twofold: Are we mature enough to get at least an estimate on the cost before plunging; and seeing it, are we then willing to go ahead? We don't know how early in his ministry Jesus saw the shadow of the cross; he probably knew from the beginning that he was always in serious danger. But we do know that when it came, it was no surprise to him; he knew, had taken into account the inevitability of it, and carried through consistently. The question is both redundant and irrelevant: " If I had to do it over again, would I do it that way? " Yet it is a question we ought to ask *before* the events, so that we are willing, at least, to take the consequences. What is even worse, the vast majority of our decisions have consequences, many of them painful, for other people. And that's a cost we have to reckon with.

A college professor found that the work of one of his students was falling below par. This student was a favorite with the faculty and was being considered for a major scholarship award at graduation. In fact, the word had come through the department head to give the boy a green light because he made a good public relations image for the school. If the prof gave the boy a " C," the whole academic shooting match would have been lost, but a " B⁻ " would have gotten by without too many fireworks. Actually, the student's work was a " C⁻ " or below in this particular course. An interview with the boy proved unsuccessful. The teacher spent a long night weighing the consequences, which included in his imagination as dawn came, the possible loss of his job for departmental insubordination. Believing that there was somewhere a mysterious righter of all wrongs, that justice always won out, and that moral courage somehow was always the best, he wound up giving the lad a " C⁻." Retaliation proved to be worse than he could have projected, the professor's career was crippled, and he is bitter about it to this day. " Would you have done it differently? " some ask. " I don't know," he muses sadly, " I don't know." He hadn't anticipated his own sardonic reaction to the irony.

Saul Alinsky, executive director of the Industrial Areas Foundation, is causing much concern among those who have always felt that loving acts are gentle and socially approvable. Mr. Alinsky is a specialist in community organization in those neighborhoods where people live in deprivation, poverty, or prejudice. Because such communities tend to spin off the top, the leadership that has come to accept the acceptable, Alinsky feels that to identify and " shake out of the bushes " the natural leaders who remain, he must address them in a language that only the resentful and rejected would understand. This includes a barrage of scorn for the " establishment," a spirit of contention against city hall, the use of a vocabulary not ordinarily heard in Sunday school, and an amassing of power that usually frightens the " power structure " out of its wits. When he was recently interviewed at an airport concerning a certain city whose underprivileged were on the verge of violence, he flaunted a package of diapers in the faces of the press, saying they were the only equipment the city council was fit to wear. There was evidently some kind of implication that the venerable councilmen were infantile. Church people were shocked and the paternalistic do-gooders were indignant.

Actually, Alinsky wasn't talking to them. He wasn't trying to encourage the comfortable ruling classes to believe that the poor would stay in their places like good children. He was using a highly effective and emotionally communicative way of talking to the very people with whom he was most concerned: the poor. It didn't matter to him whose feelings he injured or what good taste he violated; he was sending a message by the press that was heard loud and clear in the slums. And they said to each other: " He understands us. We can trust him. He hates those sonsabitches as much as we do."

His next steps in such a project, if we can judge by his record over thirty years, would involve bizarre and impudent demonstrations, organized picketing of industrial and political power centers, and generally undignified portrayals of the human suffering so long ignored. Suffice it to say that in his wake there have been no riots, no organized crime or even civil disobedience, instead, responsible problem-solving and increased participation in civic matters. His tactics are offensive but not harmful, startling but not destructive. These are consequences he well knows and takes into full account — a cost worth being paid.

Alinsky has irresponsible counterparts and competitors. Extremist groups make political hay out of emulating him without considering the cost. Black Muslims and communist exploiters alike sow hatred in his wake, hoping to capitalize on the ruins of the devastation that they stimulate. But by maintaining his consistent optimism that all people " have a chance," he has held open the doors of freedom for thousands to walk through at their own speed.

By way of review, this chapter has outlined the component parts of an ethical decision: (1) finding out the real scoop about man and deciding what it means for *me*; (2) adopting a strategy of love that sees man in specific, in the setting of other men; and (3) doing what has to be done. Augustine wasn't too far off in saying that when we love God, we should then do as we please. For then we would please to please God.

# 5

---

## THE REAL SECRET:
## MORAL PERSONS

SOME CALL it the "new morality." As though the twentieth century has discovered some vast secret hidden in Holy Scripture for years! Or worse, as though some modern scholars have purposefully distorted the Bible, reading Einstein's relativity into it and coming up with a denial of decency and morals!

Neither is true. It isn't new. It wasn't new in Jesus' day, though he livened it up a bit. It's older than the prophets of ancient Israel. When David laments, "The sacrifice acceptable to God is a broken spirit; a broken and contrite heart, O God, thou wilt not despise" (Ps. 51:17), he has advocated exactly what we are talking about.

It is dangerous, of course. Many people will listen to the description of freedom and hear only the license to do that which is right (or expedient or fun) in their own eyes. But to get the full perspective on what it means to be human, we just have to take that risk. Jesus did.

There are those who read into the current discussions of morality a "decay." "It seems that all the old teachings are being shrugged off, and the world is getting worse. Just look at our teen-agers!" "Decay" is probably a good word, for changes are taking place in value structures. Take a walk through a grove of redwoods along the California coast. Towering hundreds of feet into the air overhead are the giants of all plant life, trees taller and stronger than most city skyscrapers. But notice also that the process of life which raised the mighty heads of the trees is also a process of decay. The forest floor will be covered several feet deep with rotting branches, twigs, needles, bushes. Thus is the ground enriched, and thus sprout the little green shoots which centuries later will be up there with the biggest trees. Decay, that is, the reordering of what was once the receiver of living nourishment and now, in death, contributes to that nourishment, makes for the life and change that keep the woods in dynamic and stately growth. The one constant, the absolute, is life itself. The forms of life come and go, grow up and fall down, decay and re-form. Specific trees in the forest look different, but the overall appearance is the same.

So it is with the dynamic of love. Love itself, or morality if you please, is absolute. The supremacy of the relation that honors and deals justly in freedom and respect with all men never changes. But expressions of the relation, patterns of behavior and ways of obedience, do change, and here the process of development and decay does take place. In our Western society it is considered a bit " queer " for men to hold hands together; in the Orient it is common practice. Is one right and the other wrong? moral or immoral? Our culture ascribes a particular morality to monogamy; Muslims and nineteenth-century Mormons could have plural wives. My Protestant forebears considered dancing, drinking, smoking, using cosmetics, and reading the paper on Sunday to be especial affronts to God; they don't offend many of us now. The " rightness " of all these things is concerned with the flow of genuine love, not the act.

A generation ago a girl who " got into trouble " was disgraced for life and her family made a community laughingstock. Now she is a certain " social problem " and part of the " milieu of our times "; she frequently returns to finish school, at least accepted, and sometimes a heroine. Wrong? It is possible that our treatment of her is more humane and therefore more loving; it is also possible that we are too weak to face the long-range implications and our gentleness is only avoiding the real moral issues involved. It all depends on the circumstances.

Go ahead, call it the new morality if you want. Its only real newness is the novelty of basing an ethic on authentic inter-personal love instead of law, and that is so rare that it is always new. But you will find it all there in the Sermon on the Mount.

The Sermon is probably an accumulation of several teachings of Jesus, restated by the Gospel writer from memory and tradition. It is still rather remarkable as a document to know. Found in Matthew, beginning at the fifth chapter, this series of sayings needs to be approached from the standpoint of being an " in-family " consultation. Without a sense of personal commitment to a revolution in personal relations, a sense of the majestic in persons, and an awesome respect for the limitless aspects of love, the Sermon on the Mount could be inane or even dangerous. It is not a set of rules to live by; it is an exposure of love's potentials in illustrative form. It is an intimate conversation between the Master and his friends with whom he has been living for some time and has developed a close relationship of trust.

It is overdramatic to say that Jesus claimed there was a secret to morality. He didn't go in for little games like that. Yet, for him even to discuss morals as person-centered instead of law-centered was to catch his hearers off base. While the people of his day were frantically trying to ward off the feelings of guilt that a legal system seemed to fire at them all the time, Jesus calmly and matter-of-factly said that the whole issue was not *morals* but *moral persons*. And since the famous Sermon is the clearest and most complete of his recorded remarks on that subject, it is good that we look at it here.

The Beatitudes set the tone for the words that follow. Probably a hymn or poem used frequently by the disciples, it describes lyrically the developments along the path to emotional maturity and faith. The word " blessed " means that the person has been given a fortunate advantage, has had an unexpectedly happy development by being conscious of these unheroic traits in himself. By looking closely, you can also see a dynamic progression, an unfolding of an awakening ethic, in these little verses. Although they begin with a sense of unworthiness, there is a "lift-off" from the inert launching pad into honest and selfless involvement in the human arena.

Watch. "*Blessed are the poor in spirit.*" Perhaps better said: "How fortunate you are to be so candid with yourself." The first step toward maturity and health for any of us selfish, fragile, wondering human spirits is the realistic acknowledgment that when it comes to the things that make for purity and truth, we are poverty-stricken. We are not good, we are not God, and it's only right for us to know it. "*Blessed are those who mourn.*" Sounds contradictory? Try: "You're really fortunate if you feel bad enough about your human limitations that you look around for help." The alcoholic, for instance, begins his trip to recovery when he comes to the point where he really wants out — not before.

The momentum of the rising person is under way. "*Blessed are the meek.*" True humility is an emotional rarity. Take inventory of yourself and honestly chalk up your evaluations. Then, you will have to develop the discipline of living with your own realistic image. We are nearly ready to orbit into ethics. "*Blessed are those who hunger and thirst for righteousness.*" You're being downright sensible if you genuinely want to be pointed in the direction of being thoroughly on the side of humanity.

So the launching is complete. From complete negation, the growing person has rounded off into the mainstream of human interaction. Notice the complete lack of the hortatory. Jesus isn't saying "You must . . . ," "You ought . . . ," "You have to. . . ." This is a superb touch of tenderness at the place of our greatest vulnerability, for he completely avoids the guilt-provoking words. Right at the level where we are so frightened of any kind of accusation, the Master opens a door and offers a nonthreatening invitation. " Your own timidity can be the beginning of happiness." This is the way the gospel is offered, and can yet be the way the church proclaims it to the world. Not " Be moral, you selfish monsters! " but, " Don't be afraid to be honest with yourself. Humanity is our predicament too. We are brothers."

So, with the first four little verses, we are in motion. We have a good thing going, and it gets even better as the next little verses describe the characteristics of being able to love. " *Merciful.*" It's quite a discovery to wake up and find that you really care. " *Pure in heart.*" Good emotional health involves outgoing motives. It's a pleasant feeling to realize that you have strong yearnings for the welfare of other people, with no personal gain hung on as a necessary rider. " *Peacemakers.*" Perhaps the highest calling in the honor of loving is that of being used as an instrument of reconciliation.

" *Blessed are those who are persecuted.*" Sounds a little paranoid in translation, but it probably means that the dismay you will feel when you realize that the world is threatened by genuine love, and that you will have to be a nonconformist, will be offset by a sense of authenticity. This line is repeated in vs. 11 and 12.

To review: If you put yourself, by your realistic appraisal of your motives and limitations, open to God's help, you will become a person strongly able to love others. This is the starting point of morality, and you will note that it is relational rather than rule- or law-centered. It is interesting that the science of psychology, especially the therapy used in psychiatry, begins at the very same place to build what is called a " wholesome " or " healthy " or " integrated " personality. And although psychiatry has avoided making definitions of a " healed " person, it is quite universally accepted that ability to identify helpfully with others is a very important part of life.

The next two directives, concerning the salt and the light, are gentle encouragements to have an outward-turned life, communicating with confidence one's inner concerns to the outer world and engaging in courageous interaction. Salt can be mixed with sand, and light can be blown out, but neither one is meant to be hoarded. The cooped-up person who tries to live a meaningful life by himself is just as ridiculous a picture as a lamp put under a basket. Jesus didn't need to comment that a bottled-up flame would go out for lack of oxygen — his hearers were with him all the way and would have drowned out the scientific explanation with giggles, anyway.

Then, after an appreciative reference to law, in this case the accumulated experience and moral values of the religious community, Jesus carefuly instructs his followers: "Unless your righteousness exceeds that of the scribes and the Pharisees. . . ." You've got to be *at least* as concerned about God's will as are the self-consciously religious people to get even a start on genuine morality. Legal obedience, he says, is the minimum, not the most, when you truly think of others. It's the starting line, not the goal.

One great apprehension many respecters of tradition have today is that a fresh understanding of morality may bypass or even completely reject the lessons of the past. Here, and in other passages, it is made quite clear that Christian morality gets its whole direction and its powerful conscientious loyalty from the discoveries of the centuries. Followers of the gospel are in no sense "antinomians" (a technical term meaning "opposed to the law"). They probably revere the intent of the law more than anyone. The word given here is proper; any intention of being a person responsible to religious values has to start where the best of the past has come. In fact, these words complement the Beatitudes as a necessary prologue to the examples with which Jesus continues.

Now come the famous passages that start: "You have heard that it was said. . . . But I say to you. . . ." Be alert! The Master is not propounding a new code of ethics, or reinterpreting the law, or even offering a new law. He is looking at the *same* law from a humanity-directed love. He is actually putting in parallel columns the different, yet complementing, areas of emphasis between law and gospel. Law, he points out, applies directly to the *doing* of an antisocial event: "You shall not. . . ." "Don't commit. . . ." Its whole system of sanctions, punishment, and approval is based upon the things that happen among people. He, however, prefers to describe what is going on *within* the people themselves.

Since he has taken such care to give us the approach of the Beatitudes and to instruct us to witness to the world about the inner values, it is safe to say that when Jesus remarks, " But I say to you . . . ," he is not changing the value of the law but calling attention to its real corollary, the people involved. "Every one who is angry." "Whoever insults his brother." "Whoever says, 'You fool!'" He has turned the whole issue not upon the act but upon the kind of person doing or thinking the act.

This becomes a prime subject for Christian morality. Christ is interested in persons, and all moral principles are people in action. The point at which morality comes to bear is not in the commission but in the commitments of the people who are committing. The point to which this calls the attention of the faithful is what we might call the fulcrum of morality. To all legalists and defensive thinkers, the watershed of morality is whether or not the moral (or socially acceptable) thing has been done or violated. Jesus never denies that there is a difference between right and wrong, or that the law is misleading in suggesting that this is so; he just moves out of that arena entirely and into the subject of whether or not people have loving intentions.

When the question arises, "What is morality?" the first answer that occurs to most of us has to do with a description of behavior, its judgment and evaluation in the light of reason, experience, training, and a code of directives. We, all of us, in our different contexts, will repeatedly press for these directives to answer the restless wonderings about ourselves, whether we are "doing right," therefore, keeping our own self-image of "being right." From a simple job description in a factory to a list of class assignments in a college classroom to a review of the findings of the Supreme Court, our society is littered with rules and regulations that are so categorical as to give us the security of knowing how our " doing " is judged.

In this classical passage Jesus is quoted as telling us that however handy it may be to have the law around, and however efficiently the law may serve to safeguard the mutual welfare of the populace, it is not the place for a judgment on morality for those who trust the good news he brings. That place is to be found in the latent morality of persons. It is here, he contends, that we must look to find out if we are good little boys and girls; and if it is a certain security of self-satisfaction that we are after, we will have to study why we *want* to do this or that, rather than the trophies of our conduct.

The first of his comments does not deal with the question, " Is murder always wrong? " but rather with " What comprises a murder? " He answers the question most clearly, with example and documentation. Murder exists, he says, wherever anyone degrades his brother's dignity through rage, hostility, vilification, resentment, or the simple indifference of not even trying for a reconciliation. So there! If you're so interested in knowing what's right or what's wrong, look at the dynamics of what's going on in the intentions of the players in the drama. You may see a worse destruction of human life there than that which any dagger could do.

The next subject has little to do with adultery or sexual behavior and much to do with sexual maturity. To the morality of the man-woman scene, Jesus points out that it all depends on whether sexual interest can be the channel of admiration for the person as a reflection of Creation, or a post on which to scratch where we itch. The mention of the offensive eye to be plucked out tells us that any phase of our personality that tends to denigrate others in the glory of their humanity will destroy us first. And after all, we got into this whole proposition of morality through wanting to survive the entire moral question with some sense of preservation. He has pulled the rug out from under us on which we stood to receive merit badges for refraining from doing what our spoken standard of values told us not to do. So we cannot consider ourselves as sexually very virtuous if all we have done is bottle up our drives without evaluating them in line with our existence as persons.

The revealing goes on, mercilessly yet tenderly on, as Jesus unmasks the supposedly ethical in us as having little to do with morality. " Again you have heard that it was said . . . , ' You shall not swear falsely.' . . . But I say to you, Do not swear at all. . . ." If the observer had any tendency to be cynical, he could rise at this point with a cheer for the obvious twist of irony. Why protest so much that this time is for real when, if you really are an authentic person, you will communicate with honesty on all levels? Does it not imply, if you have to have every important declaration notarized with seal and signature, that what is not so embellished could properly be untrue? It is quite probable that this reference to a commandment and a tradition that concern one way by which to be sure of the truth is really a reference to the difference between legality and morality. The law-bound mentality will only trust that which is clearly under the sanction of law. The person who is committed to a life of love and respect will always be authentic. So Jesus says, " Let what you say be simply ' Yes ' or ' No '; anything more than this comes from evil."

It is in the use of the famous " eye for an eye and a tooth for a tooth " law of the wilderness that the Sermon on the Mount comes to its description of what we may rightly call " supermorality." This is the passage that many of us used as a mandate for pacifism, that great simple answer to the agonies of war and terror. And by using it as a *rule*, we vitiated its meaning as an invitation to vital relationships. When Jesus says not to resist one who is evil, he is not giving us a behavior directive; rather, he calls us to turn the relationship from hostility to a higher level. When another offends or degrades one's humanity, it only further deteriorates the dignity of both to continue the interaction there. The picture is not so much that of the dumb lamb before its shearers, or that of the teary-eyed martyr staring self-righteously into heaven as his accusers beat his flesh, but rather, that of the offender brought to a recognition he can't, even for the moment, bring to himself. Lest this sound too goody-goody, remember that Jesus did lash out with his tongue at some of his opponents, that he did drive the money changers out of the you-know-what, and that cowardice or passivity never marked the apostolic church under any of the circumstances of violence and persecution that it went through. The law says that when one is in a situation of danger one is justified in protecting oneself by using violence in return. This is the minimum to say: Do anything to survive. Jesus maintained that a situation of danger may also be a time for more than the minimum, when the most injured of personal values needs affirmation and the alienation that has brought on the enmity needs reconciliation. He did not overrule the practicalities of self-protection; he simply said there was more that might be done for the benefit of all concerned, not just for oneself.

"Turn the other cheek." Paul, in the twelfth chapter of Romans, adds to this the wry explanation, "for by so doing you will heap burning coals upon his head." Sounds rather gruesome until we realize that fire is a symbol of cleansing (see Isa. 6:6-7). These coals are the warmth of reconciliation and renewal, and the intention is not to avoid a fight but to keep an opening to communicate with another person at a critical time. True, it is pretty hard to pray for the Indians when the fort is burning, or, when being raped, to meditate on the noble potentials of the greedy aggressor. Yet it is exactly at that time when all the social inhibitions which are our disguises evaporate that, Jesus maintains, the moment of honesty comes. What you are at this time will betray your actual intentions and expose whether love is such a reality to you that those who would kill you are still, to you, your brothers. You might say that this ethic is the one that asks what you intend to be when the chips are down.

One does this by removing the methods of hurting from the scene first. "Let him have your cloak . . . ; go with him two miles. . . . Give to him who begs." Anybody finds it easy to respond to annoyances and indignities likewise. It is quite something else again to let them fall flat and ineffective, and then move in lovingly on a very different tack.

It is told of Booker T. Washington that while walking along a street one day he was rudely shoved into the gutter by an arrogant white man. Making no complaint, he quietly stood until the man was by, then resumed his place and pace. When asked if he didn't feel considerable resentment, he said, " I will let no man use me to hurt himself."

The passive resistance of Gandhi's movement is well known for its surprising effectiveness, and the so-called "nonviolent resistance" of the current civil rights movement is a testimonial to the workability of a person-centered ethic. This writer sat in a church in Selma, Alabama, during the critical days of March, 1965, and heard the orientation for the gathering multitudes on the principles of the tactic. We were told that if we saw any man being beaten over the head with a billy club, we were quickly to put our own heads in the way. Better that ten heads each be struck once than one head ten times. A necessary part of the resistance was to pray for the aggressor. "We will not let any man assail his own dignity by distorting another man's."

Later that same day I heard a sermon delivered in Montgomery, given under the title, "The Price of Beating Niggers Is Going Up." The thrust of the oration was that heretofore in the South many whites had had an afternoon's recreation by doing violence to some nearby Negro, either reveling in the returned hostility as an excuse for serious retaliation or watching the man choke back his bitterness, a surrender to the doctrine of white supremacy. "But now," said the reverend gentleman, "things will be different. Now, the white man is going to have to beat up someone who *loves* him while he's doing it. It's going to be far more costly to do it that way." Since the goal of the movement is reconciliation between black and white, the exaltation of all persons involved to their true recognition as brothers in creation, the intent is good. Whether or not it is successful will have to be judged by the passage of time, and will depend upon the continuation of responsible morality into the successive theaters of less dramatic and more ambiguous situations.

Nonetheless, one cannot write off this stand which the Gospel tells us Jesus maintained as idealistic. Jesus was not much of an idealist, since everything he said related immediately to a here-and-now framework. He felt there was no reason to delay the morality of love to a future, more protected time. He wasn't interested in protection; he was committed to loving people, and he was surrounded by them.

The subsequent teachings about loving your enemies, praying sincerely instead of theatrically, thinking about persons instead of things, living outwardly instead of introvertedly, are all quite in kind with the bold statements of ch. 5. They may be rightly summarized in the climax lines of chs. 5 and 6: " You, therefore, must be perfect, as your heavenly Father is perfect." The Greek word here suggests " becoming perfect," or involved in a process of renewal, reformation, and constant growth. And, " Let the day's own trouble be sufficient for the day." This, again, is a dynamic rather than a static invitation. We are to use each day as it comes for the stage setting of our love, and let it stand in its own judgment.

Now that we have gone through the Sermon on the Mount, it is good to reflect on its major impressions. It is amazing that Jesus could have lived among such a law-oriented people, so entrapped in a system that emphasized behavior, judgment, and punishment as they were, and been so revolutionary. If it were not for the prophetic tradition, which at least a few of his hearers knew fairly well, his words may not even have been preserved for us. It is also somewhat sobering to consider that the very movement which his earthly life stimulated — the Christian church — has fallen so frequently into playing the part of

custodian of public morality and codifier of the laws of virtue —
quite different from the direction he faced.

He is, indeed, calling for a supermorality. He insists that
every interpersonal confrontation is a moral event, and that a
real inventory of its value will be seen, not in what happens,
but in whether the precious, fragile little fragments of humanity are genuinely loved. He puts himself and his followers into
every situation as aggressive lovers and demands that the ground
rules be styled to augment the loving. He says that a society
will be appropriate when it is made up of people who look on
others with respect and admiration because of their being human, and he refuses to draw his final conclusions on the basis
of events or crimes or laws or opinions. Witness his several
parables of the Kingdom, later in Matthew. It can probably be
said that he didn't even trouble to think of judging deeds or
actions; he just wasn't looking that way. Morality is the foot-
print of moral persons, moral because they live to see the reflection of the Almighty in all men. Whatever the immediate
result of the way they do this, the reconciliation of broken
communication and ennobling maturity are the goal to which
they strive.

This is what makes the whole proposition dangerous. Because judgment no longer rests on the record, the measurable
events of what people do to each other, it can't be measured
at all! How can you carefully point out whether a man's intentions were good, or if he was genuinely loving? You can't! How
can you then come to any conclusions about the moral tone
of a society if you discount the crime statistics? Impossible!
Well, difficult, anyway. How can you teach morality if prohi-
bitions against wrongdoing aren't the most important indications?

Aha! This is where the real power of the Sermon on the
Mount comes in. Jesus didn't teach morality. He wasn't interested in being known as a guide to respectable living; his own
words make that quite clear. He was interested in moral persons. He gave no advice to those who sought guidance in moral

decisions; he identified himself completely with those who sought to be, wherever they were, the person who opened the door for the very best.

A skilled kindergarten teacher does not consider herself the guardian of behavior or the enforcer of ground rules. Rather, she relates to each little personality as a trustworthy and non-threatening friend. When there are incidents of disturbance in the class, she helps the children to see that there are better and more enjoyable ways of expressing energy and curiosity. She challenges instead of punishes; she builds up self-confidence in the insecure; she leads the little folk to treat each other with consideration because it gives more opportunity for all to grow together. Once she has to start control by wrist-slapping or shameful accusations, it would soon become the only method of communication in the room. But her goals are much higher than just a well-ordered class; she wants to give the children the experience of participation in a child society of individual responsibility and belongingness. Adults aren't *that* different from preschoolers. We all need to be treated that way, and to treat in kind.

We call it here supermorality. Perhaps what we really mean is " supermoral persons," but that term could confuse us with a wide range of images from classic philosophy to the comic strips. Jesus invited us to have an unusual commitment to the ethic of turning outward in genuine concern and reverence for all that mankind has in common. And after all, all men turn out to be rather fallible too; therefore, we can't make godlike images out of anyone with a high commitment. Even so, loving intentions prove more powerful than we trust them to be.

The scene was rather tense that day at San Quentin Prison in the 1940's when Clinton Duffy became acting warden. Resentment was high among the several thousand prisoners because of excesses and inconsistencies in their hard-time treatment under Duffy's predecessors. For many a year no warden had walked through the " yard," and everybody for miles around knew why. But it turned out to be quite a day at " Q," for one of the new warden's first acts was to saunter out into the cluttered open space full of denim-clad inmates, notebook in hand and alone, chatting easily and informally with any prisoner who wanted to complain or petition. It became a daily custom of his to relate respectfully and attentively to any man who sought him out and to give fair response. As one man, now a successful executive but then one of the " cons," said: " He made us feel that we were really human, after all. Instead of being the garbage of the earth, we went out feeling that if the world only had a small handful of men like Clinton Duffy, it was worth living in responsibly." Mr. Duffy told me over lunch one day that what a man had done never mattered to him; it was what a man *could be* that he looked for in every interview. Wasn't it John Wesley who once said that he looked therapeutically on every man he ever met?

It is this accent we hear in the words of the Gospel. And even here, it comes not so much in " teaching " as in demonstration. The Sermon on the Mount is not a chiding to us to be loving persons; it is a witness that God starts the whole thing by being who he is, as we see him in Christ, and invites us without prejudice to be loving persons alongside him. Since this all took place in history with the same ground-level circumstances with which we have to work, we see supermorality not as possible or practical but as a joyful and privileged response to the gift of life.

# 6

## SEX ON THE ROCKS

THERE'S A favorite old joke about a prim and proper lovely young Sunday school teacher who quickly and happily wound up in bed with every man she dated. When asked about the apparent moral inconsistency she answered, " I just wanted my students to know that you don't have to drink, smoke, and swear to have fun."

This story, like several thousand somewhat similar ones that we tell one another every day, carries not only a bit of spritely humor but a wistful statement of our intentions. We have suddenly rounded a corner in human development in which several unexpected circumstances make the heretofore sacrosanct sexual relationship available and almost fashionable. Our mores have long since passed our morals, and now we look at each other with an amazed blankness and say, " Why not? " Some of us gleefully throw ourselves into sexual experimentation with little hesitation; others are more problematically locked into the patterns of the past, and only wish we could do so. It is the latter who tell the risqué stories.

The trouble with opening this topic is that a discussion of the morality of sex isn't exactly what most questions are about, though they sound that way. " What's wrong with premarital intercourse? " " When I get married, why can't I continue to have the freedom of sexual intercourse with others? " " Now that there's no danger of pregnancy, why wait? " These questions sound as though they come from a genuine desire to understand the ethical implications and to apply to them a sophisticated rationale that soothes the conscience and makes us all feel good about the whole thing. The fact of the matter is that they are questions based on appropriateness rather than morality, and a thousand convincing answers will still leave a certain anomalous bewilderment in the minds of honest people. The proof of this statement can be seen in imagining what the response would be if some important and dependable authority were to give the categorical answer that *all* extramarital intercourse is wrong. Verily I say unto you, it would not be accepted.

And rightly so, because even the most hard-and-fast moralists of our day have surely come to see that the sex relationship has too many sacred potentialities to be locked up in any human institution. At the same time, the most uninhibited liberal knows only too well that the modern mind is far more easily convinced of the rightness of what it wants to do than of what it ought to do, and some of the keenest minds of all history are unleashing a chaos of complications in this field that will probably destroy more lives annually than will our fabulous freeways. Into this dilemma we can also toss the " gift " that our economy and technology have dropped in our laps, namely, the opportunity to be involved in bizarre sex confrontations and get away with them. We are not under pressure to deal with discovered consequences, nor does one indiscretion ruin a life as before.

Since, then, the stinger has been almost entirely removed from the scorpion's tail, and our dismal threats have no meaning, how do we talk to ourselves about the morality of sex when we really don't want to know so much about its reflection on our nature as how we can reap the harvest of its recreational possibilities without risking our sense of wholeness and security? Agent 007 invites us to go along with him on a fantasy adventure in espionage. Before we have been with him for twenty minutes, we have been in bed with four lovely nude cooperative young ladies — one at a time. How do we reflect on this after the picture? It's all fiction, we say. Yes, and what interesting fiction! Makes you think about the heroism of cloak-and-dagger work in a different light.

Enough of this. It does no good to raise a lament about the sexual confusion of our day, as though it has ever been any better. It hasn't. Or, as though the public shift of our teachings about sex has been downhill, and we are in a time of moral decay. Also incorrect. It is true that we live in a time when the context of our behavior has very new factors. It is probably true as well that our response to these factors has been strongly in the direction of far more activity in the heterosexual and other categories, such as homosexual, autoerotic, exhibitionist. But the question can be properly raised, and I hesitate not to raise it, as to whether there is any change for the worse in the actual " morality " of this generation. The mere fact that, when the lid was off, so much wild energy went into motion suggests that what is being released is powered by the very attitudes of a few years ago which we labeled " proper." It is true that much of what is happening today may someday be called " excessive." Few cultures have ever oriented their whole symbolism around the erotic, as we are doing today, and managed to keep their culture going for very long. Since we are (as all ages are) in a period of transition, our calling appears to be to live in our context honestly, to face the present instead of the past, and to make way for the kind of evaluation of what we are in that will pave the way for honesty in subsequent times.

So it is with sex. Practically none of the hard-and-fast rules of our fathers are held very seriously. By actual nose count of those who have been honest enough to answer the direct question candidly, more than half of the couples whose marriages I perform have been to bed before they arrived at the altar. And for most of these couples there is no remorse, no apology. It is the tenor of the times. It isn't at all uncommon for a single woman or divorcée to talk over with her clergyman the sexual performance of the men she has dated, sometimes even in advance of the event. High school folklore now discusses the love affairs of fellow students on the same level as fashions in clothes or speech. Overheard at a church youth meeting the other night when the chairman asked for a certain girl: " Oh, she's down at the lab having the rabbit test. Her period's late! "

What can we expect? A superheroic morality among our sexually curious and lonely when the idea of " chastity " is as much corny " oldsville " as Zeus himself? These people, and all of us, are only responding in kind to the conversation of our society with itself. The well-groomed, handsome young boy who takes the pretty girl out for dinner, then to a borrowed apartment for a drink, may be dealing more honestly with her, and us, when he paws her leg and asks, " Wanna make love? " than we tend to give him credit for. He is echoing the heroes around him, the lead man in the award-winning movie and the neighbor his parents like so much. Mayhap the very irate father, on learning of his daughter's loss of virginity, was so indignant that he made a pass at his neighbor's wife that very week! We're all in this together.

We have titled this chapter " Sex on the Rocks " to give the picture not of a cold drink, or an uncomfortable romance, but of a shipwreck. That damaged hulk has been scraping over the shoals for many centuries, not just lately. The rocks are not just the ones of modern libertarianism but ones of the age-old problem of clumsiness in the presence of the holy. Because the splendor is so easily blurred by our awkwardness, it will always be a salvage operation for anyone who tries to make the most of the subject in a truly moral sense. The rocks are not the demonic evil intent of bestial men who are bent on perverting a goodness for their own pleasure. The rocks are subsurface misinterpretations of self, man, family, and the all-important nature of agape love. These misinterpretations are not, in most cases, deliberate and are sometimes the very result of what purported to be a righteous morality. It is much better to talk about them than to dwell on useless accusations and lamenting breast-beatings.

Once again, we are driven to an examination of the nature of man. Nowhere does the contrast of man with his animal cousins come out so sharply as in the field of sex and reproduction. For animals, sex is a blind following of strong instincts that lead to the conception of young, and there is no other purpose. It is simply the biological contact of organisms to continue life. Even though in some forms of higher life there is a continuing association, one even approaching monogamy, as among lions, it is not so much a sexual factor as a domestic one. Sexual interaction occurs only when the female is in ovulation, and neither gender requires more than that. In the human, the reproductive function is proportionately small. Ever since any kind of interpersonal activity began, long before history or memory, there has been the realization that in the act of intercourse a man and woman say something to each other in the way of mutual confirmation which is a need quite apart from the physical drives. To man, who finds that one dimension of his mysterious, nonanimal existence is interpersonal communication, it comes as an experience beyond description that sex is a means of communication between two persons which exceeds any other language or symbol. And just as he has come to realize that his vocal cords are instruments of revelation and communication that have opened up a sense of richness, being, and interaction for him, so also has he discovered his genitals.

This is the thrust of that superbly beautiful and simple passage in the Garden of Eden story. We are told that when the fruit of the tree of life had been eaten and Adam and Eve came to an appreciation of their humanity, their first discovery was sexuality. They dressed themselves, that is, concealed their genital organs with leaves, showing that there was something about this method of communication that was too mysterious and meaningful to be taken for granted. This is probably a parabolic way of saying that somewhere in primitive society the sex relationship became so overwhelming in its power to release and redeem, and became so much a symbol of emotional involvement and interpersonal commitment, that it was reserved as a subject for wonder, fear, and taboo. Primitive men could not help seeing that when sexual intercourse occurred, there were accompanying strong feelings they could neither understand nor control; therefore, they marked it off as an area to be taken seriously. And that's what we've been doing ever since, though we have been so absorbed in erotic subjectivity that we are still a people sewing fig leaves and peeking behind them with varying degrees of adoration, hostility, greed, love, respect, panic, and loneliness.

The centuries have taught us a few things that are important, albeit incomplete. We have generally learned that sexuality can lead to a life of fulfillment, self-realization, a relation of extraordinary mutual satisfaction, and that in its domestic setting, mating carried through its several stages helps us to rotate around the different positions of life in the same way in which the planets orbit the sun. We have seen that the act of sexual intercourse is but one part of an involvement between man and woman that is meant to interlock with the other aspects, such as nest-building, childbearing, and child training, societal participation, and radiation outward into mankind of the very values that proclaim themselves so purely in bed. Thus, we have come to revere the connection between sex and marriage as a holy possibility that deserves sanction and protection. We also know that there are times in all responsible lives when the road is rocky and the ultimate goal gets very obscure, and the tendency to reflect this insecurity in our sexual behavior is a human heritage.

We have also learned that the integrity of the sexual relationship cannot be relegated to the automatic mechanics of a biological description. Just as that which actually takes place in any friendship will depend entirely on the maturity and personality characteristics of the friends, so the moral value of that which happens in sex will have to do more with the people involved than with the principle of mutual copulation. Here is where the firmly held conclusions of our generalities fall afoul. We have made an institution out of marriage because it seemed good and natural so to do. It appeared to be the best preservative for the privacy, protection, and development of what happens when a man and a woman share themselves completely. But all institutions are frozen abstracts, and organic life doesn't work out that neatly. No two trees are identical, no two fingerprints, no two personalities, though we come in comfortably generalized categories. Sexual expression, which is organic, biological, psychological, and volitional, is always entirely new, with possibilities beyond the range society can ever predict.

A young woman had suffered inhuman indignities at the hands of her cruel and psychopathic husband, among them sexual rejection to the point of making her doubt any value in herself at all. After the divorce, as she contemplated preparation for another and happier marriage, she realized that she had to make some account for the psychic damage. She found herself quite afraid to even associate with any man for fear of another rejection. So she approached an old family friend, an older married man whose counsel and integrity she admired. Bluntly she asked him to give her training in sexual response in order for her to know whether it would be fair even to consider remarriage. The friend complied (who wouldn't, nowadays?) and in careful, sympathetic tenderness brought her to her first orgasm. After three such occasions they agreed that the lessons were accomplished, and they parted in fond gratitude. She later married, confident that she was able to give herself to her husband. To that extent the experiment had redemptive results.

I have no intention of endowing this illustration with a rational moral justification. It is only used here to show how the traditional inhibitions and their explanations have had to be rearranged in the modern context. As far as the woman is concerned, the danger of an unwanted pregnancy was completely avoided by the use of contraceptive pills, to which she had become accustomed in her unhappy marriage. The anonymity of urban society had lessened the danger of a destroyed reputation to practically nil. The big risk was that of becoming, involuntarily, emotionally involved with a married man, and this they had talked through to at least a certain measure of preparation. On the positive side was a very important therapy for a painful indisposition. Concerning the man, there was indeed the commission of adultery, at least in a mechanical sense. But here again the safeguards of a culture that is beginning to look, more and more, on adultery as having the same harmful effects as a public belch lessened the danger of a disruptive scandal to his wife and children. We also have to take note of his genuine interest and concern for a person who had asked for a kind of assistance he was emotionally and physically able to give. All in all, he turns out to be a pretty nice guy, but I expose my own prejudices by having to remark that I'm not quite sure I'd want my daughter to marry one!

Such is the setting of a large proportion of the sexual situations of our day. The underlying sense of the unplumbed potentialities is still very much there, but the gentle social and technological changes have completely pulled the rug out from under most of our arguments for traditional chastity. Was there such an absoluteness to our original ideas of proper sexual behavior that now, in the face of new circumstances, we must hang on blindly to the old when it no longer holds water?

On this question we get rather little help from the Bible, for the Jewish religious community didn't have the emotional coloring of taboo or guilt in the same places we do. The Old Testament held a high idea of the man-woman relationship, dealt liberally with the idea of polygamy and fornication, and watched most of its heroes go through many kinds of sexual aberrations with a minimum of condemnation. The very fact that the New Testament never uses an example of extramarital intercourse as a case in point for any kind of morality, or lack of it, encourages us to be free at least from any major closeouts as we consider what our day has given us. This is why we can look at the lady and her accommodating friend without too much prejudgment. The Bible hasn't written her off as a total loss yet; neither need we. If we did, we would have to do the same thing for most of us.

An alert college psychology professor notices that a young man in his class shows the symptoms of classic homosexuality. In conference, the lad acknowledges a dependent relationship with his mother which has led him to suspect and fear any kind of unguarded association with women. His emerging sexual urges have therefore been inverted; he has tried to relieve them with masturbation and found himself wanting physical relationships with other males, preferably young boys. As he talked with his teacher, he demonstrated that there was yet a possibility for the development of " normality." Earlier in the year the teacher had counseled with a girl whose sexual experience was ahead of her years and who had come to accept her way of life with ego values intact. After speaking with her privately, he talked with the boy and girl together, and they came to a mutual decision that a learning experience was in order. Becoming in a sense a substitute mother, the girl took the young fellow to bed and carefully guided him in the masculine role. Since being rejected was no great threat to her, she invested only the emotional response of a teacher and interested friend until he, finding that the exercising of his acquired disdain of femininity was less important than the authenticity of the sex act, found he could relate sexually, both in adequacy and in pleasure. They parted friends.

It is quite likely that this kind of episode has been going on for many ages; a similar situation is found in James Michener's *Hawaii*. But the fact that we can look at it on the basis of its merits and its loving intentions instead of its irregularities means that we have many basic things to consider lest we become entirely libertarian, justifying everything by whether it " seems right," which would be most unwise in the field of sex.

It is true that the examples we have been using so far have

been teaching and healing ones; it is also true that most sexual episodes, especially the impulsive ones, are probably somewhat different in motive and content. This illustrates the fact that there is no such thing as a morality of sex; there is only the morality of the people involved, and the ultimate contribution of the act will come through the interaction of human lives and the ability to react with society responsibly.

It is well, then, that we take the same three factors mentioned in the previous chapter as components of an ethical decision in special reference to the subject of sexual relationships. These were (a) the nature of man and our position because of it, (b) the strategy of loving man, both in specific and in general, and (c) the appropriate tactic.

No subject so completely derives from an exploration into the nature of humanity as sex. It is that unique crossroads where the physical man, in full motion as a biological organism, enacts the mystery of being other than physical. It is the chief time when he uses the earthy to portray the spiritual. Here the writings of Pierre Teilhard de Chardin become lyrically scientific as he tells us that man only realizes his full nature as spirit-in-body in his sexuality, and that orgasm becomes to him the portrayal and the enactment of selfhood in dialogue with being. Sex is the place where complete exposure as a person is most possible, or most repressed. It is the moment at which he can fully be, or fully hide. This is why the very mentioning of generalities is fraught with ethical, moral, social, psychological, legal, and religious dimensions. And then, to get to specifics!

For anyone who is contemplating a sexual engagement, whether in fantasy or in fact, there is the necessity of coming to grips with a philosophical description of the partner and the social purposes of the act. Even the horny sailor who shacks up with the town whore is quite verbose, at least to himself if not to his buddies, about the needs to be filled and the human value to be released or suppressed. Many married men invest less of an effort in relating in some kind of interpersonal reality with their tired wives than Sailor Bill does with Flossie. Those who seek "relief" or "biological fulfillment" in sex are forthrightly admitting to seeing the sex partner as an impersonal object and, in the same moment, are confessing a certain attitude toward sexual humanity, refusing to permit the message of a transcendent humanity ever to pertain to "me." To translate: if a man treats a woman impersonally, he has revealed the way he treats himself.

This is the point where an acceptance of the Christian teaching of creation becomes important. To see in one's mate a divine complementation of all the wondrous aspects of one's own humanity is to see what God's plan means. "And the two shall become one flesh," said the apostle. "Husbands, love your wives as your own body, for anyone who loves his wife loves himself." Indeed. Whatever your attitude toward your love partner, whether lifetime mate or assignation of the moment, it is precisely your attitude toward yourself and toward all men. If she (or he) is something to exploit and despise, to adore and respect, or to play with indifferently, see in that your revealed picture of yourself. It is impossible to be so organically involved with another person without an unexpected and frequently unwanted unveiling of the psyche. If, then, yours is a high concept of the meaning of humanity, the one with whom you express the intimacy of humanity becomes the symbol and the target of a sharing in kindness, and the recipient of a giving without reserve. If, on the other hand, there is buried deep in the unplumbed caverns of your subconscious a fear or hatred of yourself, or a despising of the elements of life that others revere, then it will be revealed to you in your romantic life. This is why some of us have to embellish our sex lives with sadism, rehearsal of child roles, violence, hysteria, or utter icy silence.

As in so many cases of "discussions" or "seminars" on matters of considerable public interest, the answers that we prefer to give out do not always match up with the questions asked. Obviously it would be much more to the liking of anyone writing about the ideals and theology of sex to deliberate on the idealistic overtones. But the questions brought, especially by youth, have little to do with idealism and much to do with practicalities and specifics. It's best that we approach the subject in the way in which it's really raised.

A somewhat experienced guess would be that the primary question runs something like this: "Now that there are so many safeguards and conveniences to make the act of intercourse between consenting adults harmless, I challenge society to show me why I can't treat the matter recreationally." The question has caught us with our argumentative trousers at half-mast, for so much of our chiding toward chastity has been put on the basis of the dire consequences: unwanted pregnancies, disease, gossip, ruined life, etc.

To give an honest consideration to this challenge, the thinking person would have to start by making certain stipulations. It is true that the setting of modern ways makes participation in private lovemaking both available and organically safe. The invention of the automobile started it and Enovid finished it up. It is also true that the old wives' tales about love affairs, or assignations, or visiting prostitutes, or masturbation, or homosexual play's being harmful to the body and provoking insanity, are all museum pieces. In addition, current researchers from Kinsey on have made a strong case for the fact that many of us are already carrying on considerable nonmarital coitus with an apparently minimum load of remorse. We would also have to call attention to the fact that the legal permissiveness of marriage is no guarantee that the sexual relationship on which marriage is based is either valid or moral. Without doubt, many liaisons across history that were not blessed by formal marriage vows were blessed with a genuine and thoroughly loving interaction.

The question raised, therefore, is just as dangerously too general as the unyielding, supposed sexual mores of public life. Neither is worth discussing. Marriage can be wrong, and love outside of marriage can be genuine. But that doesn't really answer the question because the answer will always depend on the nature of the relationship itself. A high-placed executive had an attractive secretary who was somewhat shocked when he asked her one day to be his mistress, which meant being sexually available to him. She felt that he was being both greedy and capricious with her and unfair to his wife. But as the months went by and the girl noticed that the man carried heavy emotional loads with great concern for all the lives affected by his decisions, and that he had indeed been honest in his request of her, she felt more kindly about him. She felt that she did indeed want to support and uphold him and that there would be an element of a greatly creative love that she could communicate to him, as only a loving woman could. So she felt strongly inclined to reconsider her answer to the invitation.

In that she felt, when she was first asked, that the arrangement was to be primarily recreational, completely on the surface for immediate pleasure with no significant involvement of personalities, it seemed that her personhood and worth as a cohuman had been insulted. On review, she came to feel that the suggestion was more sincerely meaningful than it had seemed at first. Accordingly, she upheld her insistence on a consistent witness to authenticity and had every right to reconsider later.

Another woman found by way of a required physical examination at her work that her blood responded positively to a Wassermann test. Research showed that she had congenital syphilis, contracted from her father before birth. Her husband of twelve years disbelieved the story and accused her mercilessly of unfaithfulness, in which he was quite in error. The woman found that in resisting the barrage of scorn from him she was imbedding herself in resentment. Fearing that it would ruin her marriage and hurt her children, she decided to make the accusations come true. She approached a casual acquaintance at work, offered to pay half the motel bill, and cheerfully became an adulteress. She commented that it was like the famous story of the man who had been "executed" for murder he had not yet committed, so that when the noose broke he had it coming to him. Her resentment dissipated, she returned to her husband, smiling inwardly every time he called her a filthy name, saying: "That's right. So what else is new?"

Notice that the motive here was the maintaining of a responsible stability for the sake of the home, and draw your own conclusions.

A middle-aged man sorrowfully watched his wife become an uncontrollable alcoholic. When she finally had to be institutionalized, his best friend's wife, who had admired his patience and gentleness with his wife's problem, offered herself to him secretly as a token of love and as a way of helping him carry on his other responsibilities during his wife's absence. He was deeply and genuinely touched and understood the spirit of the offer with great appreciation. He refused the actual physical relationship, saying: "The very fact that she thought that much of me, and made the offer so purely, is all I need. To take her up on it would be to bring difficult and unnecessary emotional pressures on her own marriage. I'm glad she did it." Both acted in love, and both were blessed by the thinking of the other person.

We have started with these samples to show, by way of contrast, the usual context within which the cry for sexual liberty is most often raised. The Sexual Freedom League, with headquarters among students at the University of California in Berkeley, is made up of married and single people who maintain that society should not deceive itself by looking with disapproval upon adults who seek each other out and relate in intercourse as they feel the need. The trouble is that the group raises the wrong end of the question first. "To do it" is not the viable place to start. "To be naturally loving persons" is the real question, and how this loving maturity can be expressed to the ennoblement of all is the secondary, or tactical, question. The very fact that the question is raised the way it is prompts the observer to feel that since the concern is on freedom to do what impulse or interest leads to, it ought not even to be seriously considered.

Three sophomore girls were invited to a party thrown by the SFL, with the proviso that during the evening it would be required to take off all clothes. Curiosity more than anything else prompted them in deciding to go, and to leave when they felt it was getting too deep. As the party wore on, and garments wore off, and speeches were given pumping up the rationale for a " more moral morality," they decided to see it out. At the proper time they disrobed along with the others and were a little disappointed that the party moved directly into a physical orgy instead of a continuing intragroup communication about the honesty of nudity. The next morning, in evaluation, they all agreed that freedom and nudity could be constructive in certain parts of life, but that the underlying motives of the organization they had visited were so completely erotic that all possible beauty was clouded. Not one of the girls considered herself a prude or sexually disinterested; they just thought that physical romance had elements in it that were missing from the party. They did honestly acknowledge that if they had not gone in force, but alone and separately, each would more than likely have wound up on the bed.

A traveling businessman in a city far from home was the victim of a prank by his buddies. They hired a very attractive prostitute to be awaiting him in his hotel room one night. Though angered at first, he realized that the girl was only a professional doing her job. After having her put her clothes back on, he insisted that they sit and chat for a while. She couldn't believe that he wasn't taking her services, but she appreciated the friendly talk. " Not that I'm any saint," he said afterward, " or innocent of ever doing anything like that. It's just that I don't go to bed with a woman when it's somebody else's idea, and, besides, it was more fun getting acquainted with her top end than her bottom. She was a barrel of fun."

In a sense, there was more of the kind of morality that we are describing in this man's reaction than if he had indignantly ordered the courtesan out and excoriated his friends for their impertinence. He related in context to the people involved, on a basis that insisted on interpersonal honesty. His disclaimer, crude as some may think it to be, was a piece of high responsibility in the language of the day. Because of that honesty, it is a sample of the kind of approach that can really lift sex off the rocks.

As we said before, there are no absolute rules that pertain to every case, nor can sexual morality ever be described by the public acceptability of its behavior. But there are suggestions that can be made from the sidelines which may help those in the throes of difficult decision to know what considerations may be helpful. We have now come to the tactic, the decision on how to act. We brought to this point our view of man and our strategy of love, and plopped them down in the midst of the situation. Remembering also the two gunsight targets mentioned earlier, we can see some possibilities.

Since the inner forces that drive us toward sexual involvement are deeply interwoven with both biological need and inverted emotional needs, it is always easy, perhaps a general tendency, for us to confuse "love" with the performance of an act. Theologians call this the confusion of " eros " with "agape." The high school boy who pleads with his steady date for her to " give it " to him on the basis of showing her love is perhaps the corniest and most transparent example. His motive, rather understandable and normal for a lad his age, is the achievement of a longed-for adolescent goal, the sense of conquest and rewarded masculinity. In that he asks for it for himself, with little attention to rewards for her, he betrays the ego-centeredness of his request. He may be excused on the grounds of his immaturity, and it is very important for him and his girl friend that he gain some kind of insight into what is going on.

This transaction, however it turns out, cannot be dismissed as a bit of unfortunate and undesirable teen-age life. It is a time of high importance to them and to us. Whether or not she yields to him is not quite so significant as why she does or doesn't. A fifteen-year-old girl cannot be expected to understand the ferocious confusion of a boy's sex drives and his genuine feelings for her, or even understand herself and her own interest in intercourse. But it is possible for both of them to be in the embryonic stages of growth that may make them ask of themselves and each other what their real relationship is. If he begins to get any sense at all that sex is a powerful link between two persons who admire each other, then the stated reasons for his request will have to change. If she has even the slightest suspicion that a love act with him would be far more effective and important if it came about by a very different approach, she can, with her feminine prerogatives, bring about a more honest interaction which may be unrelated to intercourse. The fact probably is that this scene leads to defloration far more often than it needs to, and this particular opportunity for a happy development is lost in successive mediocrity.

At this crisis, this pathetic backseat demand, it is just as ill advised for the moralists to shout " No! " as for the gleefully unconcerned to cry " Yes! " The development of that minute has to be a decision that permits the greatest chances for growth, self-understanding, and the actual dynamics of maturing love. And the preparation for this decision ought to be built into the participants before the hands wander and the lights go off. One girl, whose woman's instinct told her that "tonight is the night," preceded her going out with a long chat with a married girl friend. They discussed the sex act, what it means to a woman, and what its emotional aftermaths are. As a sensible precaution, the older woman supplied the girl with a diaphragm to slip into her purse, but advised her to " think it through while you have a clear head first, because when you get all hot and bothered you won't give a damn." When her boyfriend suggested they go to a borrowed room, it was she who wanted to talk it out. "I know what you want to do, and I think I want to do it too, but I think we ought to know what we're doing." This led to a three-hour talk in a parked car and ended with a determination to " know each other better " first. Later the boy phoned the married friend to express his appreciation for good counsel lovingly given.

The scene has many variations. A married man is in constant contact with a lively young housewife because of a church committee task. The association leads to fondness and erotic attraction, and the time comes (as is almost inevitable in today's setting) when intimacy seems the most appropriate next stage. Sensing that this has come about not because of conscious plotting but by refusal to face all the issues in a realistic way, the two decide to go and see a distant clergyman and discuss their predicament. The minister wisely leads them in a review of everything they really want to accomplish, not only in their immediate romance, but in all parts of their lives, and in the roles they want to fulfill in society. He suggests that as self-determining adults they should be able to clarify to each other what the constructive and destructive elements are in their mutual attraction. Afterward, they decide to agree upon a ninety-day " cooling off " period, during which they would enumerate their goals and the consequences of the goals. When the three-month period is up, they meet again in the same minister's study to thank him for helping them make a well advised and socially responsible decision.

A young woman is engaged to her college sweetheart who is suddenly drafted and sent overseas, delaying their wedding for two years. In the interim she becomes involved with an older man, a divorced neighbor. In her loneliness she is persuaded to sleep with him; yet she maintains the front both to her family and herself that she is waiting for Ralph to come home. The moment of truth comes, and she realizes that her attraction to the neighbor is composed of short-range factors and that she does indeed want to marry Ralph, but she is afraid that she has lost the right to be his wife because of her " unfaithfulness." This is the reverse side of the usual kind of decision: she is pressed to come to an opinion of the rightness of entering a " right " marriage. Whether she should tell Ralph of her other relationship is more a matter for a " Dear Abby " column and not relevant here. The real issue is her sense of having a committed sexuality for the man she loves. In that she considers it from this standpoint, her approach has moral possibilities. And, in that she wants the best for her husband, the marriage could be a very rewarding one.

There are probably three kinds of sexual relationships, though in saying even that we should not get too dogmatic about the sharpness of the dividing lines. There are those liaisons in which there is a minimum of interpersonal involvement; there is a midrange where the act is accompanied by some kind of enabling but temporary friendship, and there is the deep mutual commitment. It should also be pointed out that in any contact, one of the partners can be operating at a different level from that of the other partner.

The first kind of relationship is typified by the one-shot visit to a prostitute by a man whose only interest is physical satisfaction. This type can also be seen in the one-night pickup in which the pair don't even take the trouble of exchanging names but go to bed, or the bushes, with no other interaction.

George L. was driving home late one night when he saw a nice-looking woman stranded by the side of the road with a flat tire. He stopped, fixed the flat, followed the woman to her home, had intercourse with her on the front seat of her car in the garage, and went on his way without exchanging more than a dozen words. Later he saw the woman in the neighborhood market. She acted as though she didn't recognize him. Perhaps she didn't.

The insights of maturity look upon this kind of episode with puzzled wonder. If this is the way perfect strangers can relate, with actually no intimacy of any kind other than mutual masturbation, what symbols do these very same people have left by which to demonstrate the actual interpersonal intimacy we all seek? Or, is it possible for some to use " silent sex " as a shield to ward off the very invasion of privacy that a genuine relationship always brings? It may be true, as one articulate harlot said, that "some men just have to get a piece of tail somewhere that doesn't boss them around. It makes them better men." And in so saying, this woman may have a more worthy motive than many less concerned wives. She may be distantly related to the minister who says what his people want him to say to make life more tolerable for them and professionally rewarding for him. But it does seem that the opportunities for a loving revelation of the truly human are minimal in this category.

The second kind of relationship may, numerically, represent the largest group in our day. Because of the presence of a certain element of casualness, of the freedom to have intercourse without the concomitant freedom to become partner to all the responsibilities of the act, something seems quite out of kilter to the serious thinkers of our day.

A doctor makes a house call on the teen-age daughter of a divorcée. As the mother is showing him to the door, she quietly suggests he return the next day while the girl is in school. When he comes to the door she has lunch waiting, and over dessert she makes it rather clear that it would be most refreshing to him and a delight to her to go to the bedroom. Afterward, interpreting what is going on to each other, they agree that it is an arrangement of convenience for him to drop around any time he wants, "no strings attached." At last report, the arrangement has continued for over two years, with house calls occurring from one to four times a month. There is a minimum of telephone conversation, and no questions asked about his wife or her boyfriends.

Or, the housewife and the milkman: it's not entirely fiction.

Or, there is the " affair," in which the members of the cast, one or both of them married, never do intend to divorce and come together in marriage, but just string a good thing along as far as it will stretch. And if it snaps, it snaps. Whew!

It is in a review of this stage that there is most confusion among the behavioral scientists and religious leaders alike. There has been much speculation on whether fairly healthy people can be involved in a sexual relationship of any meaning at all and come out of it unscathed. The Pavlovian school insists that it is a mark of maturity for people to be able to get into associations and out of them responsibly and be quite able to start all over again. Other schools feel that an authentic sexual partnership exposes the vulnerable, and properly so, to the extent that taking such an important part of life too casually may leave neurotic damage. Neither theory has ever been conclusively proven, but the life and experience of such a distinguished and scientific advocate of free love as Sir Bertrand Russell displays emotional stresses and reactions that may be important. For the person who wants to exalt humanity, his question isn't "Should I expose myself to this?" but "Can I rightly permit this to happen through me to someone else?" In the case of the divorcée, whose loneliness and *savoir faire* can be well understood by any amateur psychologist, it appears to be the doctor who was thinking less and enjoying it more, and who could have been more concerned with the emotional aftermath on a normal, manless woman.

A high school teacher, whose wife was only a few days from delivery of their fourth child, became interested in "a fatherly way" in one of his eighteen-year-old students. He invited her into his home to act as baby-sitter and mother's helper. Within a week intercourse occurred with the girl, and on the eve of his wife's labor pains, he and the girl left town. When they were accosted by the police in another state (who told him of the birth of his son), he averred that he intended to come back all the time, and was just helping the girl over a hard time in her life. Moreover, he blamed the officers at great length for ruining his little scheme by returning him forcibly to his wife when he would have surely come back under his own steam in a few days, anyway. Unfortunately for him, he was forced to make these statements in the presence of the girl, who became irate. "How could you!" she screamed. "How could anyone sleep with me and not pledge himself to me for all eternity?"

That's a good question, sister. It's one that many women cry out, and to some extent, all women, at some time or other. And, as a matter of fact men ask it too. How can anyone undergo complete exposure, the revealing of the most fragile, the sharing of the otherwise unshareable, and not be bound in a covenant from then on? The suspicion is that those who do, and the number is legion, do so at some cost. It may or may not be costly to them; it is more likely to be costly to their partners. It most assuredly is costly to society, which imagines and depends on a degree of interpersonal trustworthiness that means there is something about us that resembles what we tell each other we are.

This may be the dynamic of the phrase that appears as the words of Jesus in the Synoptic Gospels: "Every one who divorces his wife, except on the ground of unchastity, makes her an adulteress; and whoever marries a divorced woman commits adultery." (Matt. 5:32; Luke 16:18; Mark 10:11-12.) Since we have already pointed out that Jesus had no intention of laying down a new set of laws, we have to shrug off the traditional interpretation of these words as giving moral justification for divorce. Rather, he could be musing here on the inappropriateness of sharing the marriage bed, and that it does, indeed, destroy the valid relationship.

There is the story of the farmer who won a brand-new Oldsmobile in the town raffle. He didn't want the car, didn't know how to use it, and yet was too embarrassed to refuse it. So he parked it behind the barn where the cows could scratch their itching hides on the door handles. We modern car enthusiasts would look at this with pain in the you-know-what, saying, "What a waste!" This is how the sensitive person looks at sex aside from commitment.

This brings us properly to the third kind of relation, that in which there is commitment. Ordinarily we think that this occurs only or always in marriage, and not otherwise. It may be that this assumption has obvious cobwebs. Most of the contemporary, standard brand Protestant denominations are restructuring their theologies of marriage to eliminate the automatic "This is God's idea" implication. Heretofore, it has been assumed that marriages performed by the church were without question genuine, binding, permanent in divine intention even if it didn't work out that way on earth. " As Thou hast brought them together by Thy providence, sanctify them by Thy Spirit." We now know that there is *nothing* that happens at the altar that will guarantee an honest marriage; it is up to the genuineness and resiliency of the partners alone.

We *hope* that it happens in marriage, that it is at its best in marriage, and that the sacred covenant of the marital vows continues to be the actual setting for loyalty and mutual honor. We talk sincerely about God's " establishing and sanctifying marriage for the welfare and happiness of mankind." We know that marriage is not meant to be a pleasure or a privilege, but a duty to which we are called to give unwavering loyalty and priority. Yet, we must honestly admit that marriage is the best arrangement we can produce for the best to happen, and only that. What happens will depend.

We notice that the New Testament never legislates marriage as though it is an inviolable law in itself. In the fresh, functional mood of the apostolic church, it is not marriage that is held sacred but the ennobling loyalty of the partners that is the substance of marriage. If you look, for example, at the apostolic word to the married in the writings of Paul (Eph. 5:21-33; Col. 3:18 ff.) expecting to find directives that set the legal and practical descriptions of marriage, you look in vain. These are operative words, not definitive; they open the doors of possibility to those mature and loving enough to make the most of the marital joining to the glory of God. They are not *exclusive* words, implying a punishment or a divine disapproval for those who fall short; they are, instead, an invitation to participate in what Paul finally has to call a " mystery." " Husbands *should* love their wives as their own bodies."

This means that the fierce sanctions the centuries have developed about marriage, the traditional church's making of it a sacrament, and the accumulated "morality," which draws a black zone here, a white there, are not necessarily reflecting the Bible but striving mightily to underline the lessons of experience. To that extent, a well-advised and mature consideration of sexual intercourse *always* has to rotate around the institution of marriage or it will tend to dehumanize the ones involved. Since all institutions are exterior scaffolding holding up the outer facade of man until the inner characteristics become fast, the purpose of marriage is to provide the possibility of homes where mature responsibility finds its own.

The church, then, is committed to give it the fullest go for the greatest possibilities. It is not committed blindly to the institution of marriage as though it were automatically virtuous, nor to the condemnation of sexual honesty elsewhere. It *is* committed to honor all men, loving and serving the Lord. It *is* committed to use its fullest resources as a loving community to preserve and uphold the long-range values of the marriage vows.

A teen-age girl, in the not so unusual stage of rebellion at home, deliberately induces her boyfriend to get her pregnant. All her plans succeed when the lad "honorably" consents to marry her and take her out of the home. But since the marriage was, from its beginning, only a device for protest, and since it accomplished its purpose in bringing a new status of adulthood for the girl, she ceases to invest any further interest in it. Before the child is six months old, she finds the married state more of an inconvenience than a help. The young man, on the other hand, is becoming more interested in the developing relationship, and is making rather mature strides toward becoming a responsible husband and father. You will recognize this as one of the classic settings for early divorce. To gain the fullest of human values from this situation, the beloved community, or church, or concerned friend, or counselor, will need an open-mindedness to all alternatives, and patient endurance. The understanding that divorce is a viable possibility may help to bring a sensitiveness during the discussions to relieve pressure and encourage the couple to keep trying. If those to whom this couple goes for help are not precommitted to ironclad generalized solutions ("You have to make a go of it." "If you're not happy, get out of it while you're young"), there will be enough air space to let the proper growing motion take place. The element to be lamented here is not the girl's motives or the eventual developments; in a certain sense they are understandable. It is, rather, that so often when this happens, the best of resources, such as the presence of persons with insight, love, and freedom, are either not available or not used.

The same kind of concern that is given to the continuation of marriage needs to be given to the quality of marriage. Beyond any question, there are many who live in legal partnership who are ostensibly loyal in the sense of keeping out of other beds, but whose lives are destructive of the intention of marriage and adulterous in effect if not in fact. Just as marriage can be the place of highest human honor and service, it can also be the place of deepest hurt and most serious degradation of the holy human. Because of its "locked in" aspects, marriage is probably the most used arrangement for the expression of despicable cruelty. Here we are called to consider persons.

An American serviceman, whose wife and daughter were in the States, found a loving mistress while on duty in Japan. When he returned home, the girl came too, to a nearby city to minister to his needs whenever he cared to seek her out. When discovery came, the wife walked out, leaving the little daughter whom the Oriental gladly took as her own. A year later the husband was killed in a training accident, and the Japanese mistress went to court to seek legal custody of her adopted stepdaughter. The investigating social worker found such a condition of deep devotion, mature motherly care, and mutual fondness that she recommended custody be granted. Where is the *de facto* marriage?

A lively, attractive, middle-aged woman whose two sons were on the verge of high school found herself the victim of her husband's professional frustrations. Failing in business, not willing to face his inadequacies, he was subjecting her to constant tirades, accusations, beatings, and frequent infidelity which he flaunted in her face. She felt that it was her place as wife and mother to do her best to understand him, to be subject to his needs, to endure the storm, and to help him back to his feet. The situation worsened in spite of her attempts, and she became desperate. " I love him," she wailed. " I want to help him, but he's killing me. He's making me a creature of hate and resentment. I so deeply need some loving attention that I'm afraid I'll fall right into the arms of any man who looks at me twice. And then I'd feel far worse than ever." The traditional advice to such a person would be, " Go home and stick it out." It is quite possible that he who gives this woman counsel has the freedom in love to help her save her own integrity and, perhaps, her life in several ways, by putting human values before institutions.

The commitment of marriage is a covenant. Covenants can't be institutionalized successfully. The words " I love you " are not validated by a certificate on the wall. A covenant is always voluntarily made, and its lasting value depends only upon the consistent and binding maturity of those who volunteer. That there are valid marriages in our time is a glorious fact; that they are undoubtedly a minority is a less happy truth. In the richest county in California in 1965, there were 985 marriage licenses issued. There were 984 divorce cases filed. Only two thirds of the complaints got to court, and some of the licenses were unused; therefore, it would not be very scientific to make much of a statistic of these figures. (A .001 batting average? Horrors!) But it can be said that in this county there is a considerable turmoil in too many homes. It's not that marriage is failing; that is too impersonal a statement for the church to make. It is that many people are sexually and emotionally on the rocks, and the ministry of a loving and pastoral community is more relevant now than ever before.

The word of the church, then, in the light of its Biblical insights, is a lively one for today's permissive age. It probably comes equipped with a far more enthusiastic, even " earthy," gusto for sexuality than any other community; the physical as a gift of creation is superbly meaningful to us. The sense of reverence for personhood-in-sex invites us to a wider freedom than other approaches afford, because the potentialities of mystery found in one authentic, exposing, consistent relationship that loves, interacts, creates, and endures, much more deeply confirm our humanity than bed-hopping ever can.

This is where the supermorality can come to its fullest flower. Here is where the presence of truly human persons in a society of sexual permissiveness, living fully in those relationships which bring fullness in sexuality in associations of honor and love, will be as beacon lights in the dark. It is quite possible that we are entering on a time of greater sexual morality than man has ever seen — the kind that is held together not by an accusing society but by integrity from within. In that the present atmosphere of social change, itself a reaction from Victorian restriction, offers opportunity for morality to go in any direction, there is air space for the church to witness unlimited. We have now cleared away a great deal of the underbrush of superstition and whispered folklore; we can now shout from the housetops that sex and marriage are the gifts of God and history through which we can express our sexual humanity to fullest promise.

You've got to admit that whatever happens nowadays in the way of genuine, person-honoring love between man and woman just has to be for real. No social pressure made them so. That's where the church comes in; we help people to be for real. And that's why the new age is here.

# 7

## REVERBERATIONS

THE FIRST Reverberation: *Guilt*

Jesus treated guilt as a disease. He released people from their crippling feelings of remorse and inadequacy in the same way that he healed their sicknesses and handicaps.

The church has occupied the double, almost schizophrenic, role of accuser and expiator. We have sounded the themes of morality and obedience so loud and long that there is none righteous, no not one. Then we have made sure that a process for forgiveness is found in every branch of the church, from the confessional booths along the walls of Roman Catholic churches to the printed prayers of confession in the worship bulletins of Protestants.

Guilt is sickness, and sick people have inflicted it on others as a measure of control and intimidation. In any discussion of morality there has to be at least a mention of where the natural human reaction of regret for failure fits into the picture. Even to say "Love is the only ethic" is to strike lightning bolts of dismay into the hearts of those who fear that they cannot love, or don't want to, or are threatened by a purity they don't want. And no matter what is suggested in the way of appropriate procedures in life, some measure of guilt will be provoked like foam in the wake of a boat. So enters intimidation.

For some years I studied the clarinet, taking lessons under a skilled professional performer. The Boehm method of fingering was an improvement over the Albert system and required some new rules. For instance, my teacher adamantly insisted that it was "wrong" to slide the right little finger from the C key up to the E flat. An alternate key was provided for the left little finger, and one ought to see such an interval coming and get one's fingers ready to do it as the designer of the instrument had planned. My teacher would hit my knuckles with a pencil if I "cheated" in playing a passage and slid my little finger from C to E flat, or from C sharp to B natural, or if, in a chromatic scale, I ever did a cross-finger jump, such as F to F sharp, without using the right index finger side key. I became quite a moralist about these things, and later, while playing first chair in a high school band, I made those students playing in my section finger "properly." It became quite a thing to me. One day while I was playing a solo, the demonic thought struck me that I would like to know what it felt like to "cheat." So I did — I cheated right there before God and everybody. I felt unclean for days.

The ridiculous extreme of this little to-do came years later when I had abandoned the idea of being a professional musician for the simple reason of complete lack of talent. I traveled some miles to hear a clarinetist play with a major symphony. Studying him through binoculars as he played with virtuoso brilliance, I caught him "cheating" in his fingering. It certainly brought no blemish to the music; he was so skilled he could have reversed hands and played just as well. I was so disillusioned, however, that I was nauseated and had to leave the hall before the concert was finished. I even went through a backwash of guilt that because I had done it once in an amateur situation I had contributed to the moral downfall of a great, but now discredited, musician. Does it sound childish? It is. Something like the eight-year-old boy in New York who took a swing at a metal lamppost with a hammer, and at the moment of impact the lights went out. It happened to be the colossal Northeast blackout of November, 1965. No one can convince the lad now that he isn't responsible for the whole incident.

A young, successful engineer lost his wife by cancer. In great distress he came to his pastor to confess his terrible hidden secret: on his father's deathbed, his father had made him promise to become a minister, and the promise hadn't been kept. The young man was startled when the pastor not only said there was no reason he should have entered the ministry but also that there was no connection between the unkept promise and the wife's tragic death. It took several months of psychological counseling and theological instruction to wash the guilt out of his system and enable him to continue in his present profession.

When a fifty-year-old woman was killed by a violent and unexpected accident in her own home, her recently married daughter came to her minister to announce that it was she who was responsible for the death because she had become pregnant before marriage and had had an abortion. The disease of guilt would have destroyed the young woman's life if it hadn't been revealed and reviewed with competent help.

Guilt is the bruise on the sense of well-being that is the result of accusation of fault and failure. Frequently, as in the two instances above, it is self-imposed by a masochistic personality. In other cases it is pounded in from outside. Inasmuch as it is a bruise, it is a sickness and needs to be healed. A Christian view of morality attacks this bruise from two sides.

First, it propounds a kind of relationship in which the accusation is minimal. It is one thing to say, " You are guilty," as a legalistic system must say; it is quite another thing to point out honestly the alternatives of self-evaluation. In the classic parable of the Pharisee and the publican, Jesus indicates the difference. The Pharisee is the supporter of the idea of law and obedience, guilt and innocence, worthiness and rejection. So his stance in worship, though it was right for him to be there, was dishonest. He had to inform God of his purity, and wind up underlining it by putting his foot in the face of the publican. This humble gentleman, on the other hand, with no resentment against his accuser, was simply openly exposing himself to God and trusting in the understanding mercy of the Almighty to accept him. Obviously, the Pharisee was trying to shout down his sense of guilt by offering evidence that it wasn't so; the publican wasn't caught in self-rejection, but trusted that the truth, whatever it was, would treat him mercifully. Jesus' comment was that the latter was " justified," a theological term meaning being acceptable.

We can take it as a good working thought that anything which pushes a man out of the circle of feeling accepted by God and himself is sickness and needs to be resolved. Since legalism dwells upon the actual tactic for its judgments, it tends to reject those persons whose performance is faulty. Even in the case of Judas, whose actual betrayal was yet to come, there is a tenderness and acceptance in the words of Jesus: " What you are going to do, do quickly." It is because of his own self-accusation, certainly not the scorn of the apostles, that leads Judas to suicide. And at the most dramatic point of all human history, when on the cross he could have been vituperative and made all of us feel irretrievably unworthy, the cry of the Master was, " Forgive them, they don't know."

This is why Satan is important in Christian thought. He is a valuable character in the register of important people for Christians to know about. In the developmental stages of religious knowledge it was the healthy who realized that a hostility target, a kicking post, was necessary. The figure of Satan comes into theology out of the psychodynamic need of an emotionally maturing religious community. If you were to say that he is a personalized projection of man's sordid nature, you would be respectable on all sides of the theological fence since those who want to believe that he's still around as a forceful reality have nothing standing in their way. For those who understand that as we go through life there are times when our little souls just can't bear an overload of poison and have to have somebody else to turn the attention on ("He did it. It's all his fault!"), there can be a passing salute of gratitude to the idea of Satan. It is the mark of a mature adult that he no longer needs someone to blame for his own peccadilloes; it may be that the Christian church can come to the measure of self-acceptance in which it doesn't have to keep kicking old Satan around. But for those who still need him, have at it! It's far more ethical to hate a mythical figure than one's neighbor, or wife, or boss, or self.

It is in the insistence on an order of things in which the perishable spirit of belongingness in all of us must not be destroyed that the most ethical of all attitudes stands on the side of man. There are many forces that can hurt him, warp his ability to see his value in the universe, impair his courage to be. One of the most serious of these is his loss of a sense of appropriateness, adequacy, cosmic citizenship. Guilt, among such other bruises as fear, insecurity, depression, is one of those infections that, when it attacks one man, hurts the whole race. An aura of reverence for the real essence of humanity is that in which we can accept each other as we are and remain allies against the common infections. This idea may be illustrated in our resistance against certain physical diseases. For quite a time tuberculosis was an affliction of which most people were ashamed. It was a dread secret in the household where it occurred and, like leprosy, was a deliberate social hazard. He who became tubercular felt that he had to retreat from his society; society was not only against his disease, it was against *him*. Now we have come to a position of recognizing that TB is an enemy to all of us, and we stand on the side of the infected against his own infection without accusation.

It is so with "sin." Jesus always stood beside the offender, helping him to overcome his own offense, never stripping him of his dignity, always substantiating his humanity. Guilt tends to isolate and alienate; love tends to reconcile and heal.

Is there no place for remorse, or what theologians call "peni-

tence "? Of course there is. Genuine regret for the consequences of injustice is a necessary part of maturity. Assuming
responsibility for the unhappy consequences of our ill-advised
actions is one of the aspects of love. But there is a vast chasm
of difference between a fairly honest appraisal of damage done
with reparative determination, and the ego-crushing depression
of guilt. One assembles the ruins of a mistake into a scaffolding
for a new attempt in the future; the other lays a crippling despair upon any possibility of renewal. Anyone who goofs badly
goes through a sad inventory of what happened, but a healthy
person needs immediately to shrug off the morbidity of any
reflection upon his ability to stay alive.

In this line, guilt is related to the kind of self-injury that is
seen also in feelings of inferiority, failure, inadequacy, incom-
pleteness, nonbeing. Repentance is related to a realistic review
of the elements of will and circumstance that contributed to
the wrong, and to a commitment to the most loving ways of
repair.

A very competent and well-liked professional man suddenly
" went off his rocker," committed a bizarre major crime, and
wound up in prison. One of his college classmates went to visit
him. The prisoner told his friend that he had never felt a part
of the human race since he had, at an early age, overheard his
mother make a remark to a neighbor about his ugliness. All his
life he had sought unusual approval, by hard work and exceptional attainment, just to be able to live with himself. In a way,
his misdeed was a challenge to the world: " Here I am, lonely
and miserable. I want to be accepted; if you can recognize me
as human after the inhuman thing I have done, maybe I will
feel a person after all." He found, in friendships, family, and
psychiatric consultation, the belongingness he sought, and this
man is now a leader in the business community and in the
church.

The second aspect of ministry to the problem of guilt, after
the setting of a climate of support and recognition, is that
which is historically called the " forgiveness of sins." In this,

the ceremonial or symbolic part that is seen in most acts of public worship is the continuing assurance to community and individual that there really is such a possibility as forgiveness. Existentially, forgiveness is not an event but a living truth. There are times when the truth is more evident, when our need to have our alienation healed is more consciously upon us. But the fact is that a process of forgiveness is always under way in the order of life, and again, love is its evidence.

A housewife confessed to her closest friend that for fourteen years she had lived with the terrible memory of a sexual indiscretion when her husband was out of town. Instead of dealing with it, she had repressed it, and it had corroded her ability to consider herself whole. The friend suggested that the following Sunday in church she listen to nothing else but the ministerial assurance of pardon, as though God were communicating directly and personally with her. Dynamically, what was actually happening was the coming to the surface of the hidden infection, like an infested sliver's working itself out, and the sense of relief that she felt in church was the last stage in a long process. The hearing, Sunday after Sunday, of those same words of assurance for years previously had created in her the hope that it was possibly true, and the time had come for her to claim it in fact.

A nineteen-year-old boy, obsessed with dismay at his father's forceful demands for perfection at school, committed suicide. When the father came to realize what had happened, he became so distraught with guilt and grief that he nearly followed suit. Wise friends did not conceal from him that they understood the cause of the boy's death; yet at the same time, they upheld the unhappy father with their companionship and acceptance. Taking turns to be at his side, they spent weeks with him, going hunting, talking, listening to his pained outbursts. Eventually the torrent waned; the man could talk about it objectively, and at last one day he sighed, " God, it's good to feel human again! "

But these illustrations are too neat. There are those which

exhaust any kind of understanding and put a strain on faith almost beyond endurance. The problem of alcoholism is one; it merges in a bewildering way the most insoluble of medical, moral, volitional, and character trapdoors. How can we with any integrity express forgiveness to one who cries for it now but will deny it later? What are the ethics of forgiveness when a person is trapped in a repetitive pattern that over and over again washes out the whole investment of love and concern? Alcoholism, incidentally, is only one such situation. Habitual deviation of any kind, an addictive rehearsal of suicide, manifests itself in many ways.

Sometimes we mistake sentimentalism for forgiveness. It's not always the friendly pat, the soft-spoken assurance, the heartfelt " I accept you," that is the wisest tactic of forgiveness. Some of us learn rather early to exploit tenderness to the fullest for our own ends without ever really giving in to it. It's all still a matter of tactics. With some addicts, a " get tough " policy will spell the end of artificial tolerance and force a more realistic inventory. Since there is no magic treatment, one can remember, while doing all possible to find a workable tactic, Jesus' admonition to forgive " seventy times seven," and keep trying, keep trying, keep trying. There is no other alternative in love, though there may be alternatives of tactics in love. But who ever said that God deals in simple answers?

A college president, under severe pressure to keep the money-raising going and the faculty happy, became a serious drinker and then an alcoholic. The board of trustees, frequently embarrassed by his drunken public appearances but appreciative of his devotion and ability, were in a quandary. Some suggested that he be given a quiet " medical leave " for treatment. But he hadn't asked for treatment; in fact, he continued to deny that the problem was serious. Others were for sticking it out, hoping he would " come to his senses " and pull out of it. His closest friend, the president of the board, held out for a frank and public dismissal with nothing held back from the press. Messy as it was, this was the way it was done. Crushed and disgraced, the president realized his predicament and sought help. He and the board chairman remain the closest of friends.

It is of the genius of the morality of Christ that it is always at war against those things which degrade. It is also in that same genius that the Christian church carefully identifies the degradation and separates it from the humanity it seeks to exalt. Such is the case with guilt. Two events in the story of the apostolic church become archetypes for us here. The first, found in Acts, ch. 8, is the story of Simon Magus, who saw in the new church a good thing and tried to capitalize on it. He saw not so much the intent as the effectiveness of the church in its dealings with people and their problems, and thought that if he got into the act, he too could get results and, incidentally, not a little cash. So, in true accord with the values of the world in which he lived, he sought to bribe the apostles. Perhaps it would be nicer to say that he offered to buy generous shares of stock in the new enterprise. " But Peter said to him, ' Your silver perish with you, because you thought you could obtain the gift of God with money! . . . Your heart is not right before God. Repent therefore of this wickedness of yours, and pray to the Lord that, if possible, the intent of your heart may be forgiven you. For I see that you are in the gall of bitterness and in the bond of iniquity.' "

Here the apostle saw that a potentially great man was afflicted by a greed that prevented him from seeing the real ministry of the church. It was an offense that was indeed shocking. Yet Peter, without an unjust condemnation of the man, calls a spade a spade. He identifies the mistake in all its horror and then calls upon Simon, who is the only person who can do anything about it, to do it for his own sake. It is a pastoral admonition in the face of an insult to the church and a degradation of his own self. Of course, we don't know very much of the context, or the other contributions of the Christian community toward this conversation. In that it is recorded for us, we have to assume that there were witnesses and that the event had considerable significance in the church's appraisal of its own early history. All of this makes even more impressive the response of Simon, whose answer is a positive one: " Pray for me to the Lord, that nothing of what you have said may come upon me."

Forgiveness, then, does not mean the " forgetting " or the passing over of the wounding circumstance. Somebody has to identify it, preferably the offender himself. This is why the church cannot retreat into rosy generalizations, and beam with a happy and assuring smile on all suffering mankind as though " Everything's going to be all right." Just as hurt and degradation come in specific packages, so the acknowledgment of the love that heals also has to come in identifiable events. But forgiveness, as we have said before, is not an event but a lasting reality, and that's where Simon sought it.

The other incident, which has to be reviewed without a happy ending, is that of the couple Ananias and Sapphira, told in Acts, ch. 5. It seems that they also tried to participate dishonestly in the life of the early church but, unlike Simon, were not so naïve as to let the apostles in on their strategy. They *said* that their commitment to the church was total, but it really wasn't, and they thought they could carry it off. However, when they were exposed publicly their sense of shock and guilt was so strong it proved fatal. This story seems to be somewhat out of place, for at first glance there is an element of harshness that is inconsistent with the rest of the events of those early days.

Yet, it does belong because it exposes the undeniable reality of the destructive aspects of conflict. A house divided against itself, or a man who deceives himself, is the most miserable of all forms of life. Since guilt is a form of conflict, the inclusion of this story is a statement in the early days of the life of the church of the seriousness of guilt and the necessity to combat it. It can indeed be fatal; there is a part of the essence of survival that all doctors know, called the " will to live," which has no organic connection. This will can be crushed and destroyed, and many are the times when it is the only explanation for death.

One cannot but wonder at the failure of the church to save the lives of Mr. and Mrs. Ananias. Then a second wonder is the lack of any recorded remorse or regret on the part of the church that some people in its midst not only failed to make the grade but lost their lives, especially when it is noted that the passage immediately following this account describes the therapeutic ministry of the church in glowing terms: " and they were all healed."

All these passages serve to point out the utter honesty and realism of the new community of faith and of the memories of those who wrote the record. There was a sense of great urgency about the church then, a feeling that time was of the essence and that the things which were really important needed to come out. Of course, Christians are on the side of humanity for humanity, but when it comes to those who are the victims of their own psychopathic guilt, that inner privilege to choose to be well or sick is not invaded, and all that the church has to offer will not wrest away the decision to die.

It is part of the mystery of masochism that it throws a wrench into the gears of a neat ethic of love, or a healthy alleviation of guilt, or an effective code of law and punishment. There is a characteristic of human personality, latent in most but active in some, which makes us fly in the face of all existence. Historians will ponder for centuries the hidden motives of a Napoleon who would bankrupt all Europe to march to certain defeat, of a Hitler who would predetermine his own bunker suicide by hopeless decisions years in advance, of a Bruno Hauptmann, or of a Lee Harvey Oswald. We cannot dismiss them simply with the excuse that they were sick, for their sickness is also a part of us and a discouragement to morality. It is for the Christian to contemplate the even more mysterious reality of forgiveness, in fact, the whole miracle of healing of any kind, which puts before him a dramatic parable of the love that it is his calling to reflect in all that he does. This is the greater mystery.

Evidently, God leaves many open ends for us, and invites us

to play a far greater part in the possibilities of love and morality than we have ever expected of ourselves.

### The Second Reverberation: *The Risk of Love Over Law*

We may as well voice the fears of those who look upon a morality of love as being dangerous and unrealistic. The minute anyone suggests that there is a realm of justice that must, in certain situations, overrule law or custom, visions of anarchy appear all over the place. What's law for, anyway, if it can justifiably be laid aside? Where are the standards of morality that society has leaned on all these years?

These are quite good questions. Laws are written to control and protect society from hurting itself; they are not despotic enemies of the people, standing in the path to a happier life. Any man who puts his judgment above the law does so at a very considerable peril of playing God and bringing more injury to himself and others than he ever intended. It can probably be said correctly that no man has the right to declare his wisdom to be more than that of the gathered experience of the ages. If he does, he puts himself in the presumptuousness that is to the political world what blasphemy is to the religious.

In using the term " open-end morality " we honestly haven't been advocating anything that resembles capricious irresponsibility, or freedom to violate a single precept of law or decency. We have said only that love has its own ways for which no generality can be complete or binding. We have seen in the New Testament an intensive passion for opening to every man the doors that lead to intimacy and honesty with the human race. Morality isn't extralegal; it is *more* than legal. There are at least two ways this fact comes to our attention in full and loving expression.

The first way is called civil disobedience. It refers to action taken by concerned persons in the face of what is apparently an unjust law or custom. The contemporary civil rights movement has resorted to this tactic often enough to keep the rationale and its condemnations in every barbershop in the country next Saturday. When it is as well organized as it is under the Southern Christian Leadership Conference, civil disobedience comes at the end of a long list of preparatory steps, such as protest along prescribed channels, peaceful demonstrations, resort to the public and to legislators through the press, etc. When the unjust law has still not been modified, it is felt that the only thing left for those who militate for reform is to disobey the law, taking the legal consequences in such dimension as to call the attention of responsible leaders to the injustice and bring about the needed change.

The history and defense of civil disobedience is not the topic of this book. The fact is that it is one of the most effective and deeply traditional methods of reform in all kinds of systems, especially ours. It is justified on the lone and simple proposition that the state is not divine and, therefore, is fallible. Because the state is strong, as it ought to be, there are times when its errancy can be healed only by resistance, whatever that involves. To those constitutional loyalists who cry out that American democracy has its proper channels of reform built in, that recourse for any grievance is already provided for, and that there is, therefore, no opening at all to resort to disobedience, the realistic answer is, " 'Tain't so." The constitution has indeed made procedural provision for its own modification in what is probably the most careful, protective structure ever written. But providing channels and guaranteeing the responsible morality of those who expedite reform are two different things. Civil disobedience is usually directed not against that which the constitution permits but against an intransigent establishment. The favorite term is " power structure," taken from the writings of Floyd Miller who discovered that each political group has its informal and unseen board of directors who decide with what flavor the laws of the land will be interpreted. So, from the Boston Tea Party to the Montgomery March, men have been banding together in a covenant of brave disobedience to make repairs in the structure of justice for the good of all men.

Of course it's dangerous! Of course there have been those neurotics who have done all kinds of damage in gray-green clouds of self-delusion and paranoia. But since responsible action of this type always involves the assumption of all the consequences of lawbreaking, there is a selective process that makes the reformers have to have a certain element of genuine sincerity. And down through the years they have proven to be our friends. No person who practices civil disobedience has made much of a fuss to be let off; he believes so much in the law that he knows that as long as the statute is on the books it ought to be enforced. It is in the very enforcement that he hopes to make his point and bring about repeal by those who can do the repealing.

The second kind of morality that must occasionally rise above the law is what we have already described at some length: the special situation in which an immediate application of love may have to go in a different direction than the law. Here, too, we are not on a completely new subject. If you are driving on the highway and the car coming toward you suddenly veers into your path and comes right at you, you have two choices. The first is to obey the law, stay in your lane, and most probably be hit head on. The other is to violate the law by turning out of the right of way, across the double line or up on the sidewalk, and avert an accident. Nobody will seriously question your doing the latter, for everyone knows that there are special times when the law need not apply.

The ethic of love simply says that just as there are times of emergency when safety is preserved by making a special decision on the basis of the immediate circumstances, so also are there special situations when the loving expression has not been provided for in a system of law. There is no suggestion in the Bible that law is outmoded or unnecessary; there is only the affirmation that in those moments when that very man to whom God gave a startling amount of ethical freedom must put his love into motion, law need not be the final word. As a matter of fact, the same general principle pertains here as in civil disobedience, that if the law is broken, no matter how right it may have seemed in love, proper processes ought to be followed.

An orderly in a hospital took great personal interest in the patients. One elderly lady was suffering from a very painful affliction for which her doctor had been treating her with a very powerful narcotic. One weekend when the doctor was out of town, the patient had an especially agonizing relapse. The nurse could not make special use of the drug because the physician had not left orders and was out of reach. His assistant and stand-in was called to the other corner of the county on an accident case. And the poor little lady got worse, screaming in her torture for the dosage that the whole staff knew she would get if the doctor were available. Finally, unable to stand it any longer and knowing that he had the least to lose, the orderly broke into the narcotics locker, got the hypodermic, and administered the relief. In a few minutes the woman was asleep. He acknowledged his crime, was dismissed, was prosecuted for a felony, and paid a heavy fine. He knew that these were the possible eventualities of his action, but in his standard of values it was the loving thing to do.

So for those who fear that the kind of morality seen in the New Testament may be a Frankenstein's monster released on the earth to justify every man's whim, there can at least be given a calming word. We start not with the proposition that everybody is free to do what he wants, which would be the lowest possible standard. Rather, we start with law and custom as being advisory, and throw a heavy load of responsibility upon every individual to be answerable to the highest order of love. This is the highest kind of standard.

But what, you may ask, about those many occasions when, thinking he is loving but not really being that mature, a person makes decisions that bring great harm? What about lies that will make the lines of accuracy fuzzy? How secure can I feel when my high school daughter is out alone with her date, and I know from my adult experience that both of them are very self-deceptive about sexual motives?

The realistic answer is that teaching about open-end morality won't change that picture a bit. In the long run, whatever the laws of the land may be, or however strictly or narrowly we have taught them, what actully happens behind closed doors, or in parked cars, or in the marketplace, or in your neighbor's bedroom, will depend upon the moral commitments and emotional maturity of the people involved. Since this is an approach to morality that aims for the highest in loving responsibility, and since it will be contrasted in many people's minds with a system that depends on a guided obedience to rules, which is a minimum starting place, it can be derived that there is nothing to lose and much to gain.

There are, after all, certain tribal habits that stick pretty deep in our superegos and that will survive all kinds of wild deviations. After the Bolshevik Revolution of 1917, a movement of youth decided to capitalize on the Marxist teachings about traditional morality. The youth founded the League for Free Love, calling for a complete dissolution of the family and a society of scientific crossbreeding. One of their favorite demonstrations was to walk in the nude down the Prospekt Nevskiy in Leningrad every Sunday afternoon, to prove their sincerity publicly. It is interesting that this movement didn't last long, and also interesting to note that change came not only through the surprising disapproval of the Marxist doctrinarians but from inside the group as well, from those who could not abandon some of their prerevolutionary concepts as freely as they thought they could. It is also revealing that the societal reaction to this movement has produced a morality among the people of the Soviet Union of today which is almost Victorian. Even though they said that Marx's snarling denouncements of religion and morals were right, and gave approval to a government that boldly proclaimed the upturning of all traditional institutions, they never carried it off. Contemporary Russia is still rooted far more solidly in Slavic culture and Orthodox Christian insinuations than in Marx, Lenin, or Stalin, and this applies especially to individual codes of conduct.

In considering both kinds of supralegal freedom in this chapter, one has to meditate for a minute on the cultic reaction of fear and distrust that the masses give to any call to responsibility. Historically, every people has most readily accepted a regimen that demanded the least and gave the most in the way of protection and assurance. When our country was young, the liberals and world inclusionists like Hamilton, Jefferson, and Franklin were held in high suspicion by many people who thought that they were just too modern in their concepts, and whatever happened to the way our fathers did it, anyway? We see this same syndrome today in the panic that seems to strike in many hearts at the mention of the United Nations, "one world," universal government, even of civil rights, medicare, and fluoridation of the community water supply. In the church, there is the illogical but highly emotional resistance to the ecumenical movement, to church union and bureaucracy, to Biblical scholarship, and to new ways of doing things.

We're all quite alike. We prefer the safety of a proven (that is, an older) way of living to a theory that may not work out as well, or that will call from us a kind of energy or involvement that we're just not that interested in. It's a case not of "they" but of "we." Those of us who have the most to lose by change are the ones who will express the greatest fears of it and try to persuade others to hold back too.

This is what is so misleading about thinking that a manward morality is so new. True, it *is* dangerous, as the cross itself indicates. True, it does open the door for all kinds of radical creativity and permits a society of constant and rather disturbing change. True also, it puts our immature and irresponsible colleagues apparently further out of our control. But it is not new. Those who have been practicing it for years have been the very ones who were free to love and who infiltrated every frontier. They took us into rebellion and out of it into order.

They led us into Prohibition and out of it, into industrial expansion and then to the labor picket lines, to the bargaining table and higher living standards. They led us to every continent to win, join, love, uphold, blend, and respect.

It has been a very small and almost indistinguishable minority, this little band of mature lovers. But they have been there, and every consideration mentioned in this writing and in a thousand others has been theirs. Like the world at large, the church has missed seeing the crux of the Sermon on the Mount and has thought that the real practitioners were inconveniently mistaken, but in that the church has preserved and revered the words, if not in majority the meaning, it has served as a great storage vault from which, in each century, some persons have drawn the word of life.

It is now, in the turbulent and teeming twentieth century, when all the institutions that dominated the centuries are having to make major adjustments just to stay alive, that the church is rereading the lesson. It was there all the time. It has been in the church, powering the church and leading the church, for quite a while. It is the call to loving, person-centered, humanity-respecting involvement in all men's pain and possibility. There is no shadow-casting comparison here. For those who miss the point or are threatened by it, or who cannot accept it, there is honor in being obedient, so long as one is not seduced into trying to be virtuous. But for those who are willing to pay the price of being morally responsible and to take the consequences, there will be that same element of gladness which Paul reflected upon to Timothy: " For everything created by God is good, and nothing is to be rejected if it is received with thanksgiving " (I Tim. 4:4).

To them, then, and to all men, is given the same word of apostolic encouragement that Paul gave to the troublous, immature, beloved church at Corinth: " Be watchful, stand firm in your faith, be courageous, be strong. Let all that you do be done in love" (I Cor. 16:13).